T0054105

P FRONT

The theatre of resistance

Index has a long history of promoting the work of dissident playwrights, writes **MARTIN BRIGHT**

THEATRE WAS DARK and silent for more than a year and is only just blinking into the light. The pandemic represented a de facto form of censorship that took everyone by surprise – and played straight into the hands of authoritarian leaders.

Around the world, stages were empty, actors out of work. And yet some still managed to keep the flame of theatre alive even during the worst of times. The Winter 2021 edition of Index is a tribute to them.

Index has a proud history of supporting the theatre of resistance and this issue marks our determination to continue the tradition. The centrepiece of the magazine is a profile of long-time Index collaborators Belarus Free Theatre by the celebrated theatre writer and Index trustee Kate Maltby. BFT have long played a central role in resistance to the Lukashenko dictatorship and we are pleased to have been able to work together on a project to publish letters from dissidents held in Belarusian prisons over the past year.

We are delighted to publish Turkish playwright Meltem Arikan, who found refuge in the UK after being forced out of her home country by the Erdogan regime. Following the performance of Arıkan's play Mi Minör, she was accused of sparking the Gezi Park protests in 2013. She writes for us about her continuing struggles, particularly after being diagnosed with autism.

Jonathan Maitland discusses his experience of censorship and the limits of free speech on the stage in the UK.

We also publish Muzzled, a new work by Iranian playwright Reza Shimarz written exclusively for Index as a response to Samuel Beckett's Catastrophe, published in the magazine in 1984.

The situation in Afghanistan for writers, artists and journalists continues to be of great concern since the fall of Kabul in August. In the light of developments, Afghan journalist Zahra Nader, now based in Canada, calls for responsible reporting of her country by the Western media and highlights the brave work of the women journalists of Rukhsana Media, who continue to report from the country.

We also publish an extract from Hamed Amiri's memoir, The Boy With Two Hearts – now turned into a drama – which tells the story of the family's flight from the Taliban when Amiri's mother, Fariba, gave a speech calling for freedom for Afghan women.

Elsewhere, Jemimah Steinfeld interviews the Hong Kong activist Nathan Law, now exiled in the UK, about his new book, Freedom, with an extract from it published alongside.

John Sweeney asks why the Nobel Peace Prize was not given to the Russian dissident Alexei Navalny and we continue our partnership with Carcanet Books with a selection of Amharic poetry from Ethiopia.

This is my fourth and final edition as editor of Index on Censorship. I have been proud to work on a magazine I have read since I first visited eastern Europe as a young journalist in 1989. I deliver it back into the capable hands of Jemimah Steinfeld as it enters its 50th year of publication. ✖

Martin Bright is editor of *Index on Censorship*

50(04):01/01|DOI:10.1177/03064220211068678

Burning desire

MARK FRARY discusses the winter edition's cover image

The photograph on the cover of this issue of Index has a distinctly painterly feel to it, reminiscent of Rembrandt's Night Watch or a Dutch Golden Age *tronie*. Yet the work is contemporary, showing actors with the banned theatre group Belarus Free Theatre as they prepare for a production of Dogs of Europe. It is based on the novel by Alhierd Bacharevic, widely considered one of the country's most important literary works; it offers a powerful warning about the corrupting influences of dictatorship. The photo was taken by Mikalai Kuprych under the eye of BFT's artistic director and co-founder Nicolai Khalezin.

CONTENTS

Up Front

1   THE THEATRE OF
RESISTANCE: MARTIN BRIGHT
Index has a long history
of promoting the work of
dissident playwrights

4   THE INDEX:
EDITED BY MARK FRARY
Free expression around the
world today: the inspiring
voices, the people who
have been imprisoned
and the trends, legislation
and technology which
are causing concern

Features

14   WOMEN JOURNALISTS
CAUGHT IN MIDDLE OF A
NIGHTMARE: ZAHRA NADER
Many Afghan journalists –
women in particular – have fled
the Taliban or are in hiding from
the brutal regime

18   HOPE IN THE DARKNESS:
JEMIMAH STEINFELD
Nathan Law, one of the leaders of
Hong Kong's protest movement,
is convinced that the repression
will not last forever. We publish
an extract from his new book

22   SPEAKING UP FOR THE
UYGHURS: FLO MARKS
Exeter university students have
been successfully challenging the
institution's China policy, but
much more needs to be done

24   OMISSION IS THE SAME AS
PERMISSION: ANDY LEE ROTH
AND LIAM O'CONNELL
Malaysia's introduction of
emergency powers to deal with
"fake news" was broadly ignored
by the Western media – and that
only emboldened the government

28   I CAN RUN, BUT CAN I HIDE?:
CLARE REWCASTLE BROWN
Journalist Clare Rewcastle

Brown is a wanted woman in
Malaysia – and the long reach
of Interpol means there are
now few places where she can
consider herself safe

30   DREAM OF SAVING SACRED
LAND DIES IN THE DUST:
SCARLETT EVANS
Australia's mining industry is at
odds with the traditional beliefs
of the Aboriginal population
and it is taking its toll on the
country's indigenous heritage

34   BYLINES, DEADLINES
AND THE FIRING LINE:
RACHAEL JOLLEY
It's not just pens and notebooks

CREDIT: (cover) Mikalai Kuprych for Belarus Free Theatre

that journalists need in the USA, it's sometimes gas masks and protective vests, too

38 CARTOON: BEN JENNINGS
"I've done my own research"

40 MALTESE DOUBLE CROSS: MANUEL DELIA
Four years on from Daphne Caruana Galizia's murder, lessons have not been learned and justice for the investigative journalist's family remains elusive

42 "APPLE POISONED ME PHYSICALLY, MENTALLY, SPIRITUALLY": ASHLEY GIØVIK
A former Apple employee, who was fired by the tech giant after blowing the whistle on toxic waste under her office, says her fight will go on

Special Report: Theatre of resistance

46 KEEPING THE FLAME ALIVE AS THEATRE GOES DARK: NATASHA TRIPNEY
Theatre across the world is fighting new waves of repression, intolerance and nationalism, as well as financial cuts, at a time when a raging pandemic has threatened its existence.

48 TESTAMENT TO THE POWER OF THEATRE AS REBELLION: KATE MALTBY
The Belarus Free Theatre, whose 16 members have now gone into exile to escape the Lukashenka regime, are preparing to perform at the Barbican in London

51 MY DRAMATIC TRIBUTE TO SAMUEL BECKETT AND CATASTROPHE: REZA SHIRMARZ
More than three decades after Index published the celebrated playwright's work dedicated to the Czech dissident Vaclav Havel, the censored Iranian writer Reza Shirmarz has responded with his own play, Muzzled

60 WHY THE TALIBAN WANTED MY MOTHER DEAD...: HAMED AMIRI
The author of The Boy with Two Hearts on why and how the family fled Afghanistan

66 THE FIRST STEPS - ACROSS EUROPE WITH LITTLE AMAL: JOE MURPHY AND JOE ROBERTSON
Good Chance Theatre on their symbolic take on the long journey of refugees from Syria to the UK

70 FIGHTING TURKEY'S CULTURE WAR: KAYA GENC
Theatres have been shuttered in Istanbul but the fightback by directors and playwrights continues

73 I WROTE A PLAY THEN LOST MY HOME, MY HUSBAND AND MY TRUST: MELTEM ARIKAN
The exiled Turkish playwright's Mi Minör was blamed for the Gezi Park protests

76 WHERE SILENCE IS THE GREATEST FEAR: ISSA SIKITI DA SILVA
How Kenyan theatre has suffered under a succession of corrupt rulers, hot on the heels of colonial repression

78 CENSORSHIP IS STILL IN THE SCRIPT: JONATHAN MAITLAND
British theatre has lost its backbone and needs to be more courageous

84 GOD WAITS IN THE WINGS... OMINOUSLY: GUILHERME OSINSKI AND MARK SEACOMBE
A presidential decree that art must be 'sacred' has cast a free-speech shadow over Brazilian theatre

Comment

88 ELEPHANT THAT SHOULD BE IN NOBEL ROOM: JOHN SWEENEY
The winners of this year's Peace Prize deserve their accolade, but there is another who should have taken the award

92 WE ACADEMICS MUST FIGHT THE MOB – NOW: ARIF AHMED
The appalling hounding of Kathleen Stock at Sussex University is a serious threat to freedom of speech on campus

94 SO WHO IS JUDGING YOUTUBE?: KEITH KAHN-HARRIS
Accused by the video behemoth of spreading misinformation, the author conducted an experiment in an effort to understand how the social media platform polices its content

97 WHY IS THE WORLD APPLAUDING THE MAN WHO ASSAULTED ME?: CAITLIN MAY MCNAMARA
It is time for governments and

businesses to decide where their priorities lie when it comes to the Middle East

100 SILENCE IS NOT GOLDEN: RUTH SMEETH
As we enter a new year, Index will continue to act as a voice for those unable to use their own

Culture

102 THE ROAD OF NO RETURN: AZIZ ISA ELKUN
The Uyghur activist and poet, exiled in the UK, yearns for his family and friends imprisoned in Chinese concentration camps

104 BEARING WITNESS THROUGH POETRY: EMMA SANDVIK LING
Poets are often on the frontlines of protest

108 THE PEOPLE'S MELODY: MARK FRARY
For the first time, English readers can now experience the joys of Ethiopian poetry written in Amharic thanks to the work of Alemu Tebeje and Chris Beckett

112 NO CORRUPTION PLEASE, WE'RE BRITISH: OLIVER BULLOUGH
The UK has developed a parallel vocabulary to avoid labelling anyone with the c-word ... until now

The Index

A round-up of events in the world of free expression from Index's unparalleled network of writers and activists.

Edited by
MARK FRARY

PICTURED: A sickly sweet pop song by Malaysian rapper Namewee and Australian singer Kimberley Chen seems innocent enough but the lyrics mask veiled criticisms of China and young nationalists, often referred to as little pinks. The song, Fragile, also mentions Pooh, often used to mock President Xi Jinping, and has other hidden meanings. It has now been removed from China's streaming platforms and the two singers' accounts on social media platform Weibo blocked

The Index

THE WOMEN WHO CAME BEFORE

MY INSPIRATION

Actress **TRACY-ANN OBERMAN** comes from a long line of activists and is inspired by the actions of her great-grandmother, Annie

I HAVE ALWAYS BEEN inspired by the astonishing women in my family. They came to this country as refugees and built a life here from nothing. My great aunts "Machine-Gun Molly" and Sarah Portugal (who wore bright red lipstick and smoked a pipe) ran the family clothing business in the East End of London. That combination of toughness and glamour is irresistible.

But more than anyone, I am inspired by my great-grandmother, Annie. She came to England when she was 14 years old to flee the 1903 anti-Jewish pogrom in Belarus. Her parents saved her by sending her to London on a third-class package to her cousin Yetta. She got a job for a penny a week at Yetta's factory and slept on a mattress on the factory floor. I grew up with her.

She only really spoke Yiddish but she had enough English that we understood that the musical Fiddler on the Roof, which she watched endlessly, wasn't just a musical to her. It was documentary. She would tell us about cossacks coming into her village with swords beheading anyone they could find, or her family praying in synagogues with the lights off in case they were attacked.

And of course, it speaks to what's going on across the world now – being forced to flee persecution. If you leave where you come from, how do you maintain your identity, especially for a younger generation who grow up differently? And if you don't keep your traditions and customs, who are you?

There was a strong streak of socialism

ABOVE: Tracy-Ann Oberman with Annie

in my family. My grandma and uncle Alf were teenagers at Cable Street in the East End, when local people fought against Oswald Mosley's fascist Blackshirts. My grandma was 14 and stood with the dockworkers. My uncle Alf got thrown through a plate-glass store front by a Blackshirt. He was 15. I am an actress, but I have become an accidental activist in the fight against antisemitism. It is the least I can do to pay tribute to the women who came before me.

I try and do my best to honour their legacy in some of the work that I choose to do such as appearing in the BBC One drama Ridley Road or playing a female Shylock based on my great grandma fighting the fascists in 1936. ✖

Tracy-Ann Oberman is an actress, writer and activist

Free speech in numbers

10,000

Lawyer's fine in Egyptian pounds for social media "insult" of officials

103

International brands at high risk of having Xinjiang cotton in their supply chains, according to Helena Kennedy Centre for International Justice

11

Years of imprisonment faced by journalist Danny Fenster in Myanmar after conviction on various charges, including spreading false or inflammatory information

3

Days after sentencing, Fenster was released after negotiations by former US ambassador to the UN Bill Richardson

5

Number of rounds of sanctions imposed by the EU, US and UK governments on Belarus

YOU MAY HAVE MISSED

GUILHERME OSINSKI rounds up important news on free expression from around the world.

Putin's People author SLAPPed

Index has joined 18 other organisations to express serious concern at the legal proceedings against journalist and author Catherine Belton and her publisher HarperCollins.

The two defamation lawsuits are being brought by Russian businessman Roman Abramovich and the Russian state energy company Rosneft in relation to Belton's book, Putin's People: How the KGB Took Back Russia and Then Took On the West, which was published in April 2020.

Abramovich's complaint relates to 26 extracts in the book, including the suggestion that his purchase of Chelsea Football Club in 2003 was directed by Russian president Vladimir Putin. Rosneft's complaint relates to claims that it participated in the expropriation of Yukos Oil Company, which had been privately owned by businessman Mikhail Khodorkovsky. Both claims were filed in March 2021.

"We believe that the lawsuits against Belton and HarperCollins amount to strategic lawsuits against public participation (SLAPPs)," the organisations said, referring to a form of legal harassment used by wealthy and powerful entities to silence journalists and other public watchdogs.

Political opposition silenced in Nicaragua

On 7 November, Daniel Ortega was elected president of Nicaragua again – with 75% of the vote. But Ortega, in power since 2007, has been silencing the media and his political challengers. His regime arrested an estimated 39 opposition members, including Juan Sebastián Chamorro and his cousin, Cristiana Chamorro, both of whom had decided to run for president. US president Joe Biden said the election was a "pantomime that was neither free nor fair, and most certainly not democratic".

LGTBQ books banned in Spain

Spain's courts accepted a request from the Christian Lawyers' Association to withdraw LGBTQ-themed books from public institutions in the eastern province of Castellón, arguing that they were harmful to religious freedom.

With that, 32 books have been removed from public educational buildings, including titles such as Chaperos en al Vaticano (Callboys in the Vatican). Spain's librarians' association said the ban was a "step backwards for the democratic freedoms we defend".

Amnesty shuts offices in Hong Kong

The national security law in Hong Kong has forced Amnesty International to close its two offices in the region.

It shut the local section office, which provides human rights education, on 31 October. The regional office, which focuses on research, advocacy and campaigning work in east and southeast Asia, will be closed at the end of 2021.

It is now "effectively impossible" for human rights organisations to operate without fear of serious reprisals, says Anjhula Mya Singh Bais, chair of Amnesty's International Board. ✖

Ink spot: Afghan cartoonists

KHALIQ DAD ALIZADA is an Afghan cartoonist in exile. Previously his work appeared in Daily Outlook Afghanistan and The Daily Afghanistan-e-ma, two independent and, respectively, English- and Dari/Pashto-language newspapers based Kabul. They closed when the Taliban seized power in August 2021.

Khaliq was instrumental in the formation of the country's first satirical magazine, Shakhgoi. He also led community projects such as a women's health and literacy initiative. Like all cartoonists, graphic and visual artists in Afghanistan, Khaliq faces impossible conditions under the Taliban. His past activities, including pointed lampoons of extremists and fundamentalists, make him a target and his medium is wholly forbidden according to their diktat.

The Index

PEOPLE WATCH

GUILHERME OSINSKI highlights the stories of human rights defenders encountering trouble

Coque Mukuta

ANGOLA

Coque Mukuta , a human rights defender in Angola and correspondent for the Voice of America newspaper in Luanda, has been charged with abusing press freedom. This follows a report he wrote in August 2020 accusing the government of corruption.

Mukuta, who has covered protests against the government in the past, is also dealing with a "term of identity and residence" order, which forbids him from leaving Luanda for an unspecified period.

Zhanar Sekerbayeva

KAZAKHSTAN

Zhanar Sekerbayeva, a poet, human rights defender and LGBTQ activist in Kazakhstan, was physically assaulted in May 2021, along with her colleague Gulzada Serzhan.

Sekerbayeva, co-founder of Feminita, was prevented from holding an event promoting women's rights in a hotel. Then they were ambushed by a group of 30 men, including a police officer, and Sekerbayeva was verbally and physically insulted.

Alieh Motalebzadeh

IRAN

In 2017, Alieh Motalebzadeh, a human rights defender, photographer and member of a campaign to protect women who were victims of attacks in Iran, was charged with "conspiracy against national security" and "propaganda against the regime".

Active in the fight for greater gender equality, she began a two-year sentence on 13 October 2020 in the notorious Evin prison, in Tehran, where she contracted Covid. Prison officials have now cut her access to phone calls with no reasonable justification.

Ahmed Al-Shaiba Al-Nuaimi

UAE

In 2013, Ahmed Al-Shaiba Al-Nuaimi was one of the diverse group of political activists and human rights defenders convicted as part of the so-called UAE 94 trial, much criticised by international observers.

Despite a travel ban on Al-Nuaimi and his family, he fled the country to exile in the UK, where he is now an educational consultant. In September 2021, hei was added to the UAE's terror list by ministerial resolution, a move condemned by the Gulf Centre for Human Rights.

CREDIT: (People Watch) Facebook; (online protection) Robinraj Premchand; (tyrants) Panther Media GmbH / Alamy

What is next for the UK to protect journalists from legal threats?

SUSAN COUGHTRIE, project director at the Foreign Policy Centre, writes about the UK's first anti-SLAPP conference

"THE ONLY THING worse than the threat is the reality" was how journalists at the Foreign Policy Centre and the Justice for Journalists Foundation's conference, in November 2021, described being subject to legal challenges often referred to as Strategic Lawsuits against Public Participation (SLAPPs).

The first UK anti-SLAPP conference brought together almost 50 speakers from more than 20 countries, including Index's policy and campaigns manager Jessica Ní Mhainín, to talk about the use of vexatious legal threats, which have proliferated globally in recent years. Journalists described in remarkable parallels the impact of this significant, yet often hidden, challenge to their role as public watchdogs. SLAPPs are brought by the powerful and wealthy, eager to avoid scrutiny, to intimidate journalists into either not publishing or removing information from the public domain.

"The process itself is the punishment" was a common refrain. Those subject to SLAPPs are tied up in legal knots, exhausting their time, money and often mental resources. Costs are a huge factor, particularly given the decline in media revenues and that journalists are often targeted as individuals.

The UK anti-SLAPP coalition has launched a public consultation on proposals for possible legislative reform, which is open until 31 December (anti-slappconference.info). ✖

THE LATEST FROM OUR CAMPAIGNS

Index on Censorship works on a number of active campaigns around the world. Find out more at **INDEXONCENSORSHIP.ORG**

Free expression at risk in the rush to introduce new online protections

Combating the creeping spectre of authoritarianism informs much of Index on Censorship's campaigning work. From Orban's gradual dismantling of Hungary's civil society apparatus to the Chinese state's desecration of Basic Law in Hong Kong, long-accepted freedoms and rights are under daily attack for millions of people around the world.

It is against this backdrop that the European parliament is pushing ahead with its Digital Services Act, a legislative behemoth akin to the UK's Online Safety Bill. Like its UK cousin, the DSA is built around a set of admirable intentions, with supporters of both claiming they are needed to tackle hate speech, death threats and child abuse. But even the most ardent DSA supporters have been unable to make the case for new laws when there already laws to tackle these crimes in situ.

As it stands, the Digital Services Act means that something legal in one member state could be forcibly removed from the internet across Europe because it contravenes the law in another member state. There is a growing concern among

civil society groups that authoritarian leaders could use this to curtail freedom of expression, political discourse and LGBT or women's rights on every platform in the European Union.

At the same time as emboldening authoritarian governments, the Digital Services Act will also place more power – not less – in the hands of the big tech companies. The legislation as it stands appoints them as both judge and jury on what is, and what is not, acceptable online content. They will have the same powers online as courts have in the "real world", but with none of the accountability.

Index on Censorship has been pushing for fundamental changes to the DSA, leading the pan-European #OffOn campaign. A coalition of civil society organisations from across Europe, it is pushing for the protection of the fundamental right to freedom of expression online. As part of this work, Index has also highlighted the unintended consequences of the DSA as it currently stands. While the campaign message is simple – "don't switch off our online freedoms" – it is yet to find fertile ground among the MEPs shepherding the legislation through.

At the time of writing, there remains a very real danger that in the rush to offer online protections, freedom of expression and exchange of ideas are being needlessly and senselessly sacrificed.

As history has shown us time and time again, once forfeited, these liberties are often impossible to restore.

Vote for your Tyrant of the Year 2021

At the end of each year, Index launches a campaign to focus attention on human rights defenders, artists and journalists and their oppressors in the news.

Last year, we gathered messages of support for six activists and journalists in prison for their beliefs or their work shining a light on activities that restrict people's freedom of expression.

This year, we are asking for your help in identifying the Tyrant of the Year. There is fierce competition. Up for the award are (in alphabetical order): Alyaksandr Lukashenka (Belarus), Ali Khameini (Iran), Bashar al-Assad (Syria), Donald Trump (USA), Gurbanguly Berdimuhamedow (Turkmenistan), Jair Bolsonaro (Brazil), Kim Jong Un (North Korea), Min Aung Hlaing (Myanmar), Mohammad Hasan Akhund (Afghanistan), Nicolas Maduro (Venezuela), Paul Kagame (Rwanda), Recep Tayyip Erdogan (Turkey), Sheikh Hasina (Bangladesh), Teodor Obiang (Equatorial Guinea), Vladimir Putin (Russia) and Xi Jinping (China). To vote, go to **tinyurl.com/tyrant2021** by 14 January 2022. ✖

The Index

World In Focus: Afghanistan

The lives of millions of people – women and girls, in particular – changed dramatically for the worse when the Afghan capital, Kabul, fell to the Taliban on 15 August. Many people fled; others were forced into hiding

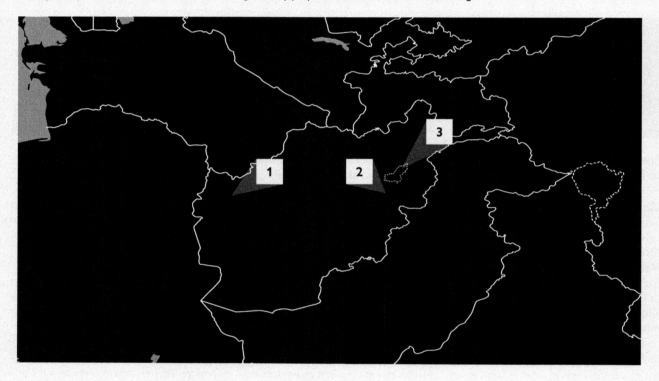

1 Herat
Journalist and university student Maryam Rezaei, 22, had quite an ordinary life until August 2021 when the Taliban invaded her neighbourhood in Herat, the third-largest city in Afghanistan.

Before that, she was one of the 10,000 women who were students at Herat University. In the meantime, Maryam Rezaei also had a job as a journalist at a local radio station. Since the Taliban's return, she has been confined to her home by strict rules that govern the lives of women.

2 Kabul
Sahraa Karimi is an Afghan film director who has produced a range of films on the rights of women and their lives in general. As a result, she became the first female president of Afghan Film, a state-run company established in 1968.

In August, as the Taliban returned to power in Afghanistan, she fled for her life. She went first to Ukraine and then to Italy, where she is now living.

Speaking to NHK World in November, she said: "If the Taliban wants to be in power, they should accept human rights, women's rights, the rights of girls to education, rights of citizens to freedom of expression, to freedom of the press."

3 Panjshir province
Fahim Dashti, 48, was an experienced journalist and leader of the Afghanistan National Journalists' Union. Known for his passionate and enthusiastic fight for the freedom of the press and highly influential among Afghan journalists, he was killed during a battle between the National Resistance Front of Afghanistan (NRFA) and the Taliban.

He had been acting as chief spokesperson for the NRFA in Panjshir province, in the north-east. A few days before his death, Dashti said: "If we die, history will write about us, as people who stood for their country till the end of the line."

TECH WATCH: FACEBOOK LOSES FACE

MARK FRARY looks at innovations with censorship and free speech implications

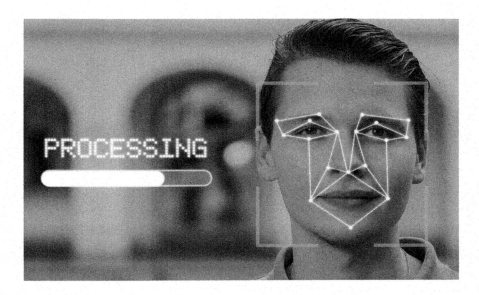

IMAGINE YOU'RE AT a peaceful protest and someone in the crowd takes a picture of the protesters, including you, and posts it to Facebook. For the best part of the past nine years, there is a chance that if you're one of Facebook's more than 1.9 billion daily active users, the platform would automatically recognise you.

While Facebook's facial recognition technology is handy for tagging friends at a social gathering, its use here is more problematic.

Facebook got into facial recognition tech in a big way in 2012 when it bought Israeli specialist **Face.com**. It doubled down in 2016 on the tech when it acquired face swapping app MSQRD and FacioMetrics.

Facebook has belatedly recognised concerns about automatic facial recognition technology and announced in mid-November that it plans to shut down the technology.

It says that the technology is used by more than a third of users and its removal "will result in the deletion of more than a billion people's individual facial recognition templates".

The potential problems inherent with the technology are evident when you look at the US company Clearview AI.

It styles itself as being "dedicated to innovating and providing the most cutting-edge technology to law enforcement to investigate crimes, enhance public safety and provide justice to victims".

It has amassed a database of more than 10 billion images of people "sourced from public-only web sources, including news media, mugshot websites, public social media, and other open sources".

Facebook repeatedly wrote to Clearview for clarification about its database while fellow platform LinkedIn sent the company a cease-and-desist letter.

An investigation by Buzzfeed in 2020 showed that the company had more than 2,200 clients in 27 countries, including the FBI, Interpol and numerous international law enforcement agencies.

In the blog post announcing the shutdown of the service, Facebook's newly rebranded parent company Meta said: "We still see facial recognition technology as a powerful tool, for

example, for people needing to verify their identity, or to prevent fraud and impersonation. We believe facial recognition can help for products like these with privacy, transparency and control in place, so you decide if and how your face is used. We will continue working on these technologies and engaging outside experts.

"But the many specific instances where facial recognition can be helpful need to be weighed against growing concerns about the use of this technology as a whole. There are many concerns about the place of facial recognition technology in society, and regulators are still in the process of providing a clear set of rules governing its use. Amid this ongoing uncertainty, we believe that limiting the use of facial recognition to a narrow set of use cases is appropriate."

Human rights defenders and activist working under authoritarian regimes will breathe a small sigh of relief. ✖

50(04):06/11|DOI:10.1177/03064220211068679

what do we know and what should we do about…?

A collection of books that offer readers short, up-to-date overviews of key issues often misrepresented, simplified or misunderstood in modern society and the media.

what do we know and what should we do about…?

immigration

Jonathan Port...

what do we know and what should we do about…?

fake news

...ead

what do we know and what should we do about…?

inequality

...ver

what do we know and what should we do about…?

social mobility

Lee Elliot Major and Stephen Machin

what do we know and what should we do about…?

internet privacy

Paul Bernal

what do we know and what should we do about…?

housing

Rowland Atkinson and Keith Jacobs

sagepub.co.uk/WDWK

SAGE
Publishing

FEATURES

"I still believe that maybe in a decade's time I can set foot in Hong Kong, when it's democratic and free"

ACTIVIST NATHAN LAW, WHO HAS CLAIMED POLITICAL ASYLUM IN THE UK, ON HIS
WISH TO RETURN TO HIS HOMELAND | HOPE IN THE DARKNESS, PAGE 18

Women journalists caught in middle of a nightmare

Many Afghan journalists – women in particular – have fled the Taliban or are in hiding from the brutal regime. **ZAHRA NADER** reports

AS A WOMAN and a journalist, I have been living my worst nightmare since 15 August 2021, the day the Afghan capital, Kabul, fell to the Taliban. Since that Sunday, I have been reporting about what women have lost – and what they continue to lose – as the new regime expands its power.

The Taliban have limited every aspect of women's lives, from banning them from school and work to introducing long black uniforms that cover them from head to toe. Having grown up in Kabul since 2001, when the Taliban were deposed, I never imagined a return to the days when women were forced to stay home because of their gender.

When I was working as a journalist based in Kabul between 2011 and 2017, the media was the last hope for dissidents. Now the media, which continue to expose wrongdoing, have turned into dissidents. Today, making an editorial decision in Taliban-controlled Afghanistan is literally making a decision about life and death.

In our small newsroom at Rukhshana Media, an all-women news website, one recurrent concern is how to tell a story with minimum risk to the people involved. The journalist is often the first to face the consequences of his or her work.

Afghanistan has never been a safe country for journalists but, after 2001, the nascent Afghan media were freer than media in neighbouring countries.

Now they can hardly function without getting visits and calls from the new rulers in charge – the group that labelled the media a military target and continued to threaten them before coming to power in mid-August. Media outlets are closing and journalists are being arrested, tortured and being forced to go on the run.

On 14 August, the day before Kabul fell, Mujeeb Khalwatgar, executive director of the Afghan media advocacy group Nai, told me his organisation had heard from journalists in Baghlan, Kandahar and Herat provinces that the Taliban were searching for them.

The same day, I talked to a young journalist from the north-eastern province of Badakhshan who said his name was on the Taliban's blacklist. He was hiding outside Fayzabad, the provincial capital.

Days before the Taliban took Fayzabad, one of his female colleagues was attacked by a man who covered his face. She survived the attack, but they were worried whether they could survive the new regime.

I talked to several women reporters from the provinces who sought shelter in Kabul as the Taliban took over, hoping to leave the country on evacuation flights. Many of them didn't make it.

In early November, a 24-year-old-woman, one of only three female journalists in an entire province – who asked me not to name the province – said she was on a Taliban blacklist, according to a relative who was working with the militants. The radio station she worked for was among more than 150 media outlets forced to close because of Taliban-imposed restrictions and the economic crisis a month after Kabul fell.

As the breadwinner of a family of nine, the change in rulers meant she not only lost her job but is on the run for her life, simply for being a woman journalist. In the past two months, she has been forced to change her place of residence seven times to hide from the Taliban.

Two weeks after the Taliban's return to power, Reporters Without Borders warned that "women journalists are in the process of disappearing from the capital". The organisation noted that, of about 700 women journalists with jobs in Kabul, more than 600 had not returned to work. Some fled while others were forced to stay at home or go into hiding.

Our investigation at Rukhshana Media shows that there are no women journalists in radio or TV working in the western provinces of Herat, Farah, Badghis and Ghor.

The systematic removal of women from the media landscape is not the only immediate consequence of the Taliban's return to power. Just three weeks after their takeover, the militants arrested 14 journalists, with at least nine of them subjected to violence during their detention, according to the Committee to Protect Journalists. Among those →

MAIN: Taliban members stop women protesting for their rights in Kabul in October 2021. "The Taliban have limited every aspect of women's lives," says Zahra Nader (portrait)

RIGHT: Female journalists are becoming a rare sight in public in Afghanistan. Here, a lone woman reporter stands out amid a forest of men at a Taliban press conference in Kabul.

→ detained were an editor and four other journalists at Etilaat Roz, a newspaper that was a winner of Transparency International's Anti-Corruption Award in 2020. Two of them were tortured by the Taliban and needed hospital treatment.

Today, journalists – both men and women – are still on the run. In November, I talked to a 31-year-old journalist who for the past eight years has been an investigative reporter for local print and online outlets. Since 15 August, he has been on the run with his family of four, having spent nights in five different places. He is particularly worried about his investigations into the Taliban-run religious schools.

"No one is listening to my calls for help, no one. I am just hoping the Taliban don't catch me alive," he said.

Reporters Without Borders and Human Rights Watch have issued warnings about the Taliban censorship of media, especially their "media regulations" which require journalists and media not to produce content "contrary to Islam" and not to report on "matters that have not been confirmed by officials".

The chief editor of a radio station in Kabul who, despite not having a passport, attempted (unsuccessfully) to get on an evacuation flight out of the country in late August, told me his story. Now he

No one is listening to my calls for help, no one. I am just hoping the Taliban don't catch me alive

is back at work, where, in one month, the Taliban have visited his office four times. Twice when his colleagues used the word "Taliban" instead of "the Islamic Emirate", he received calls warning him to be careful with the choice of words.

He says his radio station, like all other Afghan media outlets, is under the Taliban's scrutiny. Three of his colleagues in other provinces have been ordered by provincial officials to send their news first to the Taliban before it is signed off for broadcast.

With reliable sources of information having dried up and journalists either on the run or operating in an environment of fear, censorship and self-censorship, it is becoming harder to be a journalist.

The new environment creates opportunities for the circulation of false stories and propaganda on social media. Lately, it has become difficult to distinguish between real news and propaganda. Many on social media, including some journalists, are propagating stories that correspond with their biases and social and political prejudices which then will be used by some international media to verify their own assumptions and biases.

Exposing false and misleading stories has been one of the primary goals of our team at Rukhshana Media, where we investigated two stories directly connected to misinformation and staged reporting in the past two months.

Many news outlets reported that Mahjabin Hakimi, a 25-year-old professional volleyball player, was

beheaded by the Taliban. The reports were based entirely on the claim of her coach in Kabul's volleyball club who spoke under a pseudonym. But our investigation, in which we interviewed five sources, including her parents and a friend who was present the day her body was found, showed that she died on 6 August – nine days before the Taliban took over Kabul.

In the second story, several people connected to the family of a nine-year-old girl featured in CNN's bombshell report on child marriage told Rukhshana Media the report was invented.

Our reporters are working on the ground to bring women's stories to the surface of a male-dominated Afghan media. In the past months, we have partnered with two international newsrooms, The Guardian and The Fuller Project, which has helped amplify the voice of Afghan women to wider audiences outside the country.

With women journalists remaining at risk, we are trying to create opportunities for them to continue their work and tell the stories of women in Taliban-ruled Afghanistan, where they are banned from work and education and have no idea when they will be able to return to public life. ✖

Zahra Nader is an editor at Rukhshana Media (rukhshana.com), an all-women news website, and a former New York Times reporter in Afghanistan

50(04):14/16|DOI:10.1177/03064220211068680

Hope in the darkness

Nathan Law, one of the leaders of Hong Kong's protest movement, is convinced that the repression will not last forever, he tells **JEMIMAH STEINFELD**. And, overleaf, we publish an extract from his new book

PICTURED: Outside the Final Court of Appeal in Hong Kong after being granted bail in October 2017.

CREDIT: REUTERS/Bobby Yip

NATHAN LAW HAS been imprisoned, disqualified from political office and forced to seek political asylum in the UK – all for fighting for democratic rights in Hong Kong, his home city. But, in spite of it all, he remains optimistic.

"As an activist I'm not entitled to lose hope," he tells Index on Censorship. "I still believe that maybe in a decade's time I can set foot in Hong Kong, when it's democratic and free."

Law, 28, fled to London in the summer of 2020 after the passing of the National Security Law, a draconian piece of legislation that criminalises even a whisper of criticism against Beijing's rule.

Given the chance, what would he tell Communist Party leaders in Beijing?

"I would say, 'There is no totalitarian regime that can remain forever. All of them will collapse', and I'd say, 'That is your fate if you continue to do what you are doing'."

Law's face and name are synonymous with the struggles in Hong Kong. Alongside Joshua Wong, Alex Chow and Agnes Chow, he has helped drive the recent protest movement.

The son of a construction worker and a cleaner, he first became interested in democratic values at secondary school when the late writer and human rights defender Liu Xiaobo won the Nobel Peace Prize in 2010. Liu was serving his fourth prison sentence in China and was unable to accept the prize in person. An image of an empty chair soon went viral, a stark reminder of how bad human rights were in China.

"I grew up in a family that did not talk about politics, did not talk about social affairs," Law says. Although he studied in a pro-Beijing school, he was "not heavily brainwashed to believe in the Communist Party". He adds: "I was apolitical. I was not involved." But when Liu won the prize, the principal of his school publicly denounced the writer in morning assembly.

"It triggered my curiosity because I thought people getting the Nobel Prize are the ones who are good in their field. So how come such a person – a Chinese [person] – would be criticised in that fashion? It really triggered my curiosity and got me to look into the work that he had been doing. He opened up a gate for me to understand all these concepts."

That gate first led Law to the Tiananmen Square vigil, held in Hong Kong every year since 1989, and then to him leading the 2014 Umbrella Movement (which later landed him in prison on charges of "unlawful assembly").

After this, Law became the youngest legislator in Hong Kong's history, a position from which he was quickly disqualified when he modified his oath of allegiance to China during the swearing-in ceremony in October 2016.

In the same year, he founded Demosistō, a pro-democracy political party, with Agnes Chow and Wong.

But time was up when the National Security Law was passed. Demosistō was disbanded, Law was forced out of Hong Kong and Chow and Wong were jailed, alongside scores of others connected to the democracy movement.

Today, dissent is in a straitjacket in Hong Kong. And yet not all have given up fighting. In Law's recently published book – Freedom: How We Lose It And How We Fight Back – he writes: "Even during this most bitter of times the spirit of ordinary Hong Kong people continues to shine, even if it must do so in the shadows."

Law lists the people who refuse to have their prison sentences lessened by agreeing to the charges against them and instead "defend themselves in order to narrate their story at the risk of heavy sentencing". He lists those who attend →

 My message to Beijing? No totalitarian regime can remain forever

How I exposed Beijing's big lie

Young activist Nathan Law's election to the Legislative Council in 2016 shattered the myth that the people of Hong Kong did not desire freedom and democracy, he says in an extract from his new book

IN AUGUST 2016, a month before the election, our team were starting to worry. The polls suggested I had little support in the constituency I was running in. Hong Kong Island is a wealthy and generally conservative district, known for electing prominent members of Hong Kong's professional and elite class – lawyers, public intellectuals and former government officials. To make things more difficult, my constituency happened to have the highest number of elderly residents. It was also an important 'super seat' that would return six places in the legislature by proportional representation, so fifteen parties had fielded candidates.

While we were hopeful, our expectations were low. I may have been a public figure, but I was known only as a student activist. Going straight from student activism to the first tier of Hong Kong politics was not easy.

BELOW: A protester is taken away by police during one of the demonstrations against the controversial extradition bill in September 2019.

I had to adjust my mindset. I was no longer representing students like me, but having to appeal to and present myself as someone who could represent a much broader range of people. I needed to demonstrate that I had the ability to understand the complexity of realpolitik, and accommodate the diverse needs and views of constituents. I also had to convince people that I was able to represent them in the city's highest chamber. In the last two weeks of the election, I worked as hard as I could to outline my beliefs and analyse heated debates about policy. I wanted to prove that age, education and experience are not the deciding factors in what constitutes a

> **My election was a terrible loss of face for Beijing. They would not forgive me**

proper lawmaker: determination, vision and eloquence are what matter most.

The 2016 election saw an unprecedented turnout: 2.2 million voters, 58 per cent of the registered electorate, cast their vote. Despite the constant hectoring of Beijing's loyalists, the silent majority had spoken, and it was in favour of pro-democracy candidates. A new force had emerged in local politics, with new, progressive localist candidates winning six seats. And I won my seat, by a far greater margin than polls had suggested, to become Hong Kong's youngest ever lawmaker.

I was so proud of what we had achieved. We had exercised our right to stand for election, and in voting for us the people of Hong Kong had exercised their right to elect representatives who shared their concerns. The legislature may have been designed to ensure a pro-establishment majority, making it more of a debating chamber than a true law-making body. But to be one of thirty-five directly elected legislators still mattered. My election represented an expression of the limited political rights Hong Kong people enjoyed – an expression of our freedom. I had a democratic mandate and no one in government could claim otherwise. Even if all I could do was be one voice in the chamber, this voice would be heard throughout the city; and for so many people of my generation, and for all those who had voted for me, that mattered.

At twenty-three years of age, I was Hong Kong's youngest legislator. Often, babies of the House, as the youngest parliamentarians are called in the UK, go on to have long careers in politics. Mine in Hong Kong would be one of the shortest.

Legislative Council members are elected to serve a four-year term. As my team moved into our new offices in the Legislative Council Complex, there was no reason to suppose we would not be there for at least that long. We did our best to make ourselves feel comfortable in room 901. As an activist I had met and worked with many legislators, but to be sitting in the Council building now as one of them felt different. I watched political aides come and go, and my staff hovering busily about, and could not help but wonder if I truly belonged there. Was this the right place

CREDIT: Oliver Haynes/SOPA Images via Zuma Press/Alamy

for an activist? Could it accommodate us?

Well-known democratic lawmakers stopped by to welcome me. They did their best to make me feel I belonged. Many were politicians and campaigners I looked up to and had worked with during the protests. They had fought hard for a better Hong Kong – for labour rights, civil liberties and for other important freedoms. Still, any pride I might have felt was overridden by the realisation of what I was up against. Though my allies in the democratic camp were capable and respected in the wider community, they were operating within a system designed to ensure they would never have power. And those who did have power would seek to silence and destroy us.

My election had been a terrible loss of face for Beijing and their loyal supporters. It shattered one of their principal lies: that the majority of Hong Kong people are loyal patriots who place the 'nation' (meaning the CCP) over local issues and a desire for freedom and democracy. It was a lie that had served the interests of the powerful, from the officials and secret Communist Party members who dominated Hong Kong's elites to international businesses who had throughout Hong Kong's history suppressed the will of the people in order to promote so-called stability and a favourable commercial environment. It was a lie that Hong Kong's last governor, Chris Patten, had bravely challenged by going directly to the people, refusing the assurances of an elite who insisted that Hong Kong people were apolitical. It was a lie that had become increasingly pernicious as Beijing encroached on our freedoms, making democratic representation even more important. And my presence in the Legislative Council, alongside other new and progressive lawmakers, told the world that it was a lie. Beijing would not forgive me for that. ✖

Extracted from Freedom: How We Lose it and How We Fight Back, by Nathan Law, published by Transworld in November 2021

→ court hearings to show support to the defendants, those who write letters to the imprisoned and those who advocate for any policy that might remotely challenge the government.

"The hope lies in these people. Even though we are in the darkest time and change is seemingly impossible, people are still doing things because they feel that it is the right thing to do," he says.

Law might have an admirable sense of hope, but his is not an easy life. He had to publicly sever ties with his family when he moved to the UK and has been unable to talk to Agnes Chow and Wong, too. He misses the people and he misses the place.

"I always dream about Hong Kong," he says. "You're familiar with everything. You don't have to think. Like when you step into the MTR [the subway]. It's in your muscles, in your memory. You understand everything. You understand all the slang. The background noise with people's hectic walk, the hectic talk of Cantonese and bus horns, those noises from the stores and from restaurants. It's just unique."

Law has been granted asylum in the UK – a move that angered Beijing, which declared him a criminal suspect. Even though he is thousands of miles from Hong Kong, he still has to look over his shoulder. He takes extra precautions: he never mentions where he lives and he takes detours when he leaves and returns home – measures that have come to define the life of China's dissidents. He simply doesn't feel safe "because of how extensive China's reach can be".

"We've got cases like Navalny; the Russian dissident forced to land in Belarus; we've also got a lot of cases of Uyghur activists around the world being arrested or extradited back to China. There are a lot of things that can happen to dissidents. It is not a secret that I am almost at the top of the list of national enemies that China portrays, so things like this could happen," he says.

"On the other hand, I don't want any of these fears to hinder my activities and

Dissent is in a straitjacket … yet not all have given up fighting

my activism. So I will try to be vigilant to protect myself, but I will also try 100% to promulgate the agenda of the Hong Kong democratic movement."

One of the ways that he wants to do this is through publishing his book. A blend of personal experience and broader context, Law wants it to appeal to as many people as possible and for these people to "act after reading it".

"I'm an author, of course, but at the end of the day my essential identity is an activist. By definition, an activist is someone who tries to empower people to act in order to precipitate social changes. I intend to appeal to people to be more aware of their own democratic states," he says.

As for what we can do to help Hong Kong, Law puts it simply: "Get involved. Pay more attention to Hong Kong and to China. Start to look into campaigns that could help, like boycotting the Olympics, supporting political prisoners or even reading news – just supporting the news agencies who produce these fantastic stories for Hong Kong and for China.

"After that, if you really want to be a campaigner that supports Hong Kong then get organised. Find your local grassroots organisation and be a volunteer and try to explain that to your friends and your neighbours."

It might be the darkest chapter in Hong Kong's story, but – to channel Law's optimism – let's hope it's not the last. ✖

Jemimah Steinfeld is head of content at Index on Censorship

50(04):18/21│DOI:10.1177/03064220211068681

Speaking up for the Uyghurs

FLO MARKS says Exeter university students have been successfully challenging the institution's China policy, but much more needs to be done

AN ESTIMATED ONE million Turkic-Muslims are detained in mass internment camps in Xinjiang province, China, where they are subjected to arbitrary detention, forced assimilation to Han-Chinese culture, humiliation, torture and sexual abuse. While the Chinese Communist Party maintains there are only "vocational training centres", evidence from leaked state documents, satellite images and first-hand Uyghur testimony contradicts this.

On being released from the camps, Uyghurs have been subject to labour transfers away from home, with an estimated 80,000 being forced to work in factories outside Xinjiang.

The Chinese government wants to silence voices speaking out about the Uyghur genocide. But they are not the only ones. Western companies and institutions with links to the region – and therefore to the genocide – continue to quieten discussion about the issue.

At least 17 global industries have become implicated in the Uyghur genocide, from fashion to tech to higher education. The CCP has been defiant in its stance to end commercial, and even diplomatic, relations in response to criticism. This included when H&M

articulated soft concerns surrounding Uyghur cotton, which led to a Chinese-market boycott and sales falling by nearly a quarter.

Others have therefore stayed silent, but some have even gone further, such as Inditex (Zara's parent company), which denied links before a UK parliamentary committee. Its denials were instantly debunked by open-source information; Inditex did not reply to our request to comment.

With financial and academic self-interest, some renowned UK and European higher education institutions have also put up information walls and seem set on waiting for concrete evidence of their partners' and donors' links to the Uighur genocide to emerge before cutting tie. For instance, the University of Manchester (which also did not respond to our request for comment) cut its ties with China Electronics Technology Group this year only after a senior MP accused CETC of providing technology and infrastructure used in the persecution of Uighurs.

Tom Tugendhat, chair of the foreign affairs committee, said it was surprising the university had not been made aware that CETC's technology was being used to aid the atrocities. "Our letter was

apparently the first they knew of it," he said. He added: "It remains imperative that British institutions, educational and otherwise, are fully informed of who it is they are working and sharing research with."

Despite the power these companies and institutions yield, civil society and the government can, and should, hold them more accountable. Alongside the main UK Stop Uyghur Genocide Campaign, which has been hugely successful (for example in pushing Parliament to recognise the genocide and putting forward a motion for a diplomatic boycott of the Beijing 2022 Olympics), driven, dedicated and committed student activism and protests have been bringing attention to the genocide on campuses and holding their institutions accountable for current and potential complicity.

At the University of Exeter, I am involved with Students for Uyghurs (SFU). While researching the history

Despite the power these companies and institutions yield, civil society and the government can, and should, hold them more accountable

CREDIT: China News Service/Getty

The Uyghur diaspora continues to demand justice the loudest, despite the campaign of threats, intimidation and harassment

ABOVE: A factory in Xinjiang, China. Approximately 84% of China's cotton production comes from the Uyghur region

and context of the genocide, we came across the scholar Hu Angang, who is responsible for producing the ideological foundations of forced assimilation that underpins the thinking behind the internment camps and the wider genocide. He is employed by Tsinghua University in Beijing, which has partnered with Exeter and where Chinese president Xi Jinping studied.

Having become aware of this link, Exeter students launched a Freedom of Information request and interviewed staff and students. We exposed the fact that Exeter is potentially complicit in the genocide – a story which has since received national coverage in The Times. SFU is calling on Exeter to cut institutional links for ethical, reputational and academic freedom reasons.

In November, I organised and chaired an event called How Do We Prevent Exeter University Selling Its Ethics and Reputation to Authoritarian States? The university's management was commended for their sincere willingness to engage in constructive debate with students and staff over the links and the due diligence policies currently in place.

Forums such as this have been an all-too-rare occurrence at higher-education institutions. Mark Goodwin, Exeter's deputy vice-chancellor (global engagement), made some strong commitments, including that Exeter "has never and will never work with Hu Angang [...] or with questions of ethnicity", that management will further entrench due diligence relating to Tsinghua, and that it will update and strengthen (with student input) our academic freedom policy. These are all steps in the right direction.

As Jaya Pathak, chair of SFU and co-executive of Yet Again, an organisation raising awareness and understanding of modern atrocities, told Index: "This event was a fantastic example of the power of grassroots and student advocacy, and we are truly grateful to the senior management at the University of Exeter for directly engaging in an open forum to discuss the concerning relationship between Exeter and Tsinghua University."

She added: "More academic institutions in the UK must be willing to have this conversation – it is important to remember that not having physical evidence of being implicated in the crimes of the Chinese government is not a free pass to not take any action.

"Global partnerships are important, but must not be pursued at the expense of gross human rights violations, including genocide, and we will not stop holding UK universities to account for their links to the Chinese government."

Nevertheless, SFU recognises that to effect positive change, pressure must be sustained. If a red line will be drawn only when there is hard evidence then – rather than FOIs and news headlines bringing attention to complicity – information on supply chains, partnerships and donations must be published, analysed and discussed more frequently and systematically. In the case of universities such as Exeter, we believe they must now go beyond the Universities UK guidance on due diligence procedures, which has been deemed by the National Endowment for Democracy to be ineffective, and be more proactive.

The Uyghur diaspora continues to demand justice the loudest, despite the campaign of threats, intimidation and harassment being operated by the CCP aiming to silence their voices (including in Europe, as Index is investigating). But more allies are needed. To listen, amplify and embolden the brave calls for accountability of genocidal actors being made by Uighur exiles. To stand against and end the silence on potential Western complicity. And to energise discussions around this, and then turn them into action.

The recent successes of Exeter's SFU, which is in only its first year since forming, is one example of how the actions of small groups can break the silence on a subject many powerful actors would rather keep quiet, and even get some meaningful commitments. Now it's time for others to join. ✖

Flo Marks is a student at the University of Exeter and a researcher at Index

50(04):22/23|DOI:10.1177/03064220211068682

MALAYSIA FOCUS

Omission is the same as permission

Malaysia's introduction of emergency powers to deal with "fake news" was broadly ignored by the Western media – and that only emboldened the government, argue **ANDY LEE ROTH** and **LIAM O'CONNELL**

IN AUGUST, MALAYSIA was in political turmoil as a state of emergency declared in January – officially as a response to the Covid-19 pandemic – was due to end.

Facing an imminent vote of no confidence, embattled prime minister Muhyiddin Yassin deployed security forces to block opposition party members from entering parliament.

His administration faced mass protests that openly violated its lockdown orders and his opponents decried the state of emergency as a thinly veiled effort by an unpopular government to cling to power.

The enactment in March of the Emergency (Essential Powers) (No 2) Ordinance – which criminalised as "fake news" any criticism of the government's response to the pandemic and the state of emergency itself – underscored those concerns.

During the tumultuous first three weeks of August, the print edition of The New York Times published only four articles mentioning Malaysia.

Two focused on the Tokyo Olympics. None covered the state of emergency, popular protests against Muhyiddin's administration or the impact of the "fake news" ordinance. When

Muhyiddin resigned, on 16 August, the Times reported his resignation online but not in print.

The paucity of coverage in The New York Times – admittedly in a month when the world's attention was gripped by the drama unfolding in Afghanistan – reflects the broader absence of news on Malaysia, as documented by our analysis of 305 stories published by nine news outlets in the 12 weeks before and after the "fake news" ordinance issued on 12 March.

The Malaysian government is one of many to bring in emergency restrictions on civil liberties and press freedoms under the guise of addressing the pandemic. By examining patterns in international and domestic reporting on the crackdown, we show how countering censorship at a national level requires international engagement and that the international press was indirectly complicit in the Muhyiddin administration's efforts to damage recent advances in Malaysian democracy.

Fighting "fake news"?

With parliament suspended, the government enacted the emergency "fake news" ordinance without debate and even less approval. It revived →

A lack of coverage need not be the result of censorship to have negative consequences

PICTURED: Police out in force in Kuala Lumpur in August 2021 to stop the opposition from entering parliament

→ and escalated the Anti-Fake News Act 2018, which had been widely condemned for its restrictions on freedom of expression until parliament repealed it in October 2019. Officially intended to criminalise the publication and dissemination of misinformation about Covid-19, in practice it aimed to "prevent any criticism" of the government's pandemic response, according to analysis by the human rights organisation Article 19.

It empowered authorities to arrest people without a warrant and to remove online content without due process. It also created criminal liability for anyone who wrote, reported or published anything related to the pandemic that might "cause fear or alarm" and for

any media organisation, social media platform or civil society group that hosted or funded such content. We found that English-language international news outlets – including The New York Times, The Washington Post, The Wall Street Journal, The Guardian, The Economist, The Sydney Morning Herald and the South China Morning Post – never mentioned the "fake news" ordinance. In fact, they seldom covered Malaysia.

Our data included all news stories

ABOVE: Opposition leader Anwar Ibrahim in August 2021 when he was barred from parliament

published from 6 February to 23 April that at least referenced Malaysia. More than 92% of those stories published by US, UK and Australian outlets mentioned the country only in passing.

When they treated Malaysia as the primary topic, coverage typically focused on international interests rather than domestic politics. Thus,

 A lapdog on a government leash will not overexert itself alerting the public to threats

for example, on 2 March, The Sydney Morning Herald covered the impact of the 1Malaysia Development Berhad financial scandal on ANZ, a multinational bank based in Melbourne. The largest economic scandal in recent Malaysian history, one which toppled a previous administration, rated as news because it affected an Australian business.

An article in The Guardian on 20 April, on the persecution of journalists in China, noted that, according to Reporters Without Borders (RSF), Malaysia had registered "the biggest year-on-year fall" of any nation in its annual Press Freedom Index, "reflecting wider clampdowns on press freedoms across Asia".

One exception to this pattern was the South China Morning Post, based in Hong Kong, which provided more consistent coverage of domestic news in Malaysia, including the suspension of parliament and the younger generation of Malaysians "at the vanguard of resisting autocracy".

Overall, however, the international news outlets we examined failed to cover the political turmoil.

A lack of coverage need not be the result of censorship to have negative consequences. At the international level, uninterested watchdogs did little to alert audiences to the crackdown on civil liberties and press freedoms.

Lapdogs on government leashes

Within Malaysia, the New Straits Times consistently featured government officials who expressed support for the ordinance and related policies. This is not surprising because most of the country's news outlets, including the Times, are indirectly affiliated with specific political parties.

The newspaper published only one article that included dissident voices – an 11 March story on the "fake news" ordinance quoted three of its critics, including the executive director of the Centre for Independent Journalism, Wathshlah Naidu.

Limited coverage of the 'fake news' order played into the ruling party's hands

She said it would lead to "arbitrary censorships of critical and dissenting media reports, and thus, attacks on media freedom, and disproportionate crackdowns on legitimate speech".

Overall, the paper treated the government's policies as beyond reproach, a position that reflected the fundamental aim of Muhyiddin's "fake news" ordinance.

A lapdog on a government leash will not overexert itself alerting the public to threats posed by those in power.

One online domestic news outlet, Malaysiakini, courageously continued to provide a platform for opposition voices even after the ordinance went into effect.

Malaysiakini regularly quoted opposition MPs (who made up 26% of its quoted sources in our data) and civil liberties groups (24%), including international organisations (9%) such as Human Rights Watch (HRW) and Article 19.

On 13 March it published an article that included critiques by the Society for the Promotion of Human Rights and HRW. Linda Lakhdhir of HRW called on the government to revoke the ordinance because its "ill-defined terms" made it "ripe for abuse".

As a result of its opposition, Malaysiakini has regularly faced lawsuits and government investigations, but so far it has withstood the flak.

Rendering censorship less visible

By criminalising conduct "likely to cause fear or alarm" to "any section" of the public, the ordinance aimed to censor all criticism of the government's authoritarian response to the pandemic. As Article 19 noted, its "highly subjective and potentially limitless" scope would have a chilling effect, pressuring individuals and organisations

"to err on the side of self-censorship to avoid criminal sanctions".

Censorship is most effective when its operation is invisible. But while Malaysia's ordinance was no secret, the limited news coverage played into the ruling party's hands.

As research by Lance Bennett, senior research fellow at the University of Washington, the University of California, San Diego's Daniel Hallin and others has shown, the ability of the press to criticise government often depends on the range of debate among government officials.

The suspension of parliament not only left Malaysia without legislative checks and balances, it also deprived the mainstream domestic press of a fundamental source of dissenting perspectives.

This forced many Malaysian news outlets to turn to sources in neighbouring Singapore and Thailand for critical news about their government.

By ignoring Malaysia's political crisis, the international press indirectly aided efforts to silence domestic critics. Months after the administration's collapse, Malaysians continue to be charged with spreading false news.

News outlets in the USA, the UK and Australia were not subject to the "fake news" ordinance but their dismal performance in covering newsworthy events in Malaysia falls far short of the principle that they ought to vigilantly hold those in power accountable. ✖

Andy Lee Roth is the associate director of Project Censored, a US-based news media watchdog. Liam O'Connell is a student at the University of Delaware, majoring in political science and history and an intern at Project Censored

50(04):24/27|DOI:10.1177/03064220211068683

MALAYSIA FOCUS

I can run, but can I hide?

Journalist **CLARE REWCASTLE BROWN** is a wanted woman in Malaysia – and the long reach of Interpol means there are now few places where she can consider herself safe

THE MALAYSIAN REGIME is out to get me – again.

The last time it issued a warrant for my arrest, in 2015, it asked Interpol to put me on its international database under a Red Notice (terrorism) alert. This was because of my exposés about the 1Malaysia Development Berhad (1MDB) fund scandal in which about $5 billion of public money was stolen, including $681 million that ended up in the personal bank account of Najib Razak, then prime minister.

Najib responded with a crackdown, and the body of Anthony Kevin Morais, a deputy prosecutor who had drawn up a warrant for Najib's arrest, was later discovered in a submerged barrel of concrete after he was snatched from his car in moving traffic.

Therefore, I was not keen to be extradited to face charges for "activities detrimental to parliamentary democracy" and "false reporting" under draconian laws that can land journalists in jail for up to 20 years.

My reporting – in the Sarawak Report – was vindicated. The following year the US Department of Justice, working with the FBI in the Kleptocracy Asset Recovery Unit, issued one of the most comprehensive and damning civil suits in its history as it made a record asset seizure out of the proceeds laundered in the USA. The haul included a super-yacht, several prestige properties in California and New York, a private jet, billions of dollars' worth of jewellery, rare paintings and artifacts and even a movie – the blockbuster The Wolf of Wall Street starring Leonardo DiCaprio, which was produced by

Najib's stepson Riza Aziz. Consequently, at the next election in 2018, Najib and his ruling party, United Malays National Organisation (Umno), which had held on to power for six decades, were voted out. Najib was found guilty of corruption and criminal abuse of office and sentenced to 12 years in jail.

Further cases are grinding through the courts, but he remains free and is still a member of parliament – although the constitution bars him from contesting elections unless he gets a pardon or a reprieve from the monarch – pending a drawn-out appeal process that favours the rich. Likewise, several senior colleagues charged with corruption divide their time between parliament and court appearances.

Given their freedom to operate, decades of political power and enormous wealth, it is perhaps not surprising that in 2020, two years after being voted out – and just as Covid struck – Najib and his allies overturned the elected government through a series of backdoor manoeuvres and defections. After Muhyiddin Massin was pushed aside in August, Umno formally took charge of the ruling coalition and installed a close ally of Najib, Ismail Sabri Yaakob, as prime minister.

An early result of the change of political fortunes has been the steady dropping of prosecutions against Umno figures caught up in the 1MDB and related corruption scandals, along with the opening up of investigations and prosecutions into their political opponents. Najib himself has openly expressed confidence that he will soon have his own charges and convictions overturned in order to stand at the next election and become party president again.

So where do these developments leave me as the foreign journalist who exposed him and who became the target of numerous government-backed operations to intimidate and harass me at the height of the 1MDB affair from 2015-18? Najib still frequently rails against me on his Facebook page and plainly seeks to discredit and, if possible, criminalise me.

New moves against me culminated in an arrest warrant issued on 23 September this year – apparently because I did not turn up for a hearing of which I was unaware.

My immediate concern is that such charges could, again, make me subject to Interpol requests that put me in danger of arrest, particularly at border stops, even in friendly countries.

This process has interrupted the lives of numerous journalists, freedom campaigners and opposition figures worldwide, having become a favoured method by which oppressive regimes

 I'm told the Malaysian authorities are investigating me for sedition, for which the punishment is up to 20 years in jail

seek to silence inconvenient voices who have escaped their jurisdiction.

If you are arrested on foreign soil as a result of an alert slipped on to the international databases that you knew nothing about, it can take months of expensive legal support to get back home. Worse, you might be held in custody or even extradited to face "justice".

In Spain, for example, which I visit frequently from the UK, the law still upholds the concept of "criminal libel", of which I am accused in the 23 September warrant. Turkish journalists targeted in President Recep Tayyip Erdoğan's notorious media crackdowns have also been arrested on this charge.

I have been told that the Malaysian authorities are investigating me for "sedition", for which the punishment is up to 20 years in jail, and "false reporting".

When Malaysia moved against me in 2015, civil society organisations including Fair Trials and Index on Censorship protested on my behalf. And, in a rare move, the secretary-general of Interpol, Jurgen Stock, rapidly and

If you are arrested on foreign soil as a result of an international alert you knew nothing about, it can take months of expensive legal support to get back home

publicly dismissed Malaysia's request.

I was fortunate then to be involved in a high-profile case. However, I am warned that this time Malaysia may use other tactics, such as bilateral extradition requests, instead of reporting to Interpol directly.

Following requests for information on my behalf by no fewer than 14 press freedom groups, Interpol has confirmed that, so far, no request has been received from Malaysia.

But on 2 October, The Daily

....

BELOW: 'I am warned that this time Malaysia may use other tactics,' says Clare Rewcastle Brown, who has been targeted since her exposés in 2015 about the 1MDB financial scandal

Telegraph in London quoted Interpol as refusing to rule out acting on such a request in advance of receiving it.

There is a complex process that someone in my position can now go through – using specialist extradition lawyers to approach Interpol and let them know I am a target and that requests against me should be treated as suspicious – but I am advised it costs several thousand pounds and can take many months. During that time I would be at risk and even an Interpol positive vetting would not rule out co-ordination between Malaysia and other countries.

For this reason, as a journalist who writes about south-east Asia, I already avoid visiting countries with which Malaysia has close co-operation.

So I now have to gulp and hope if I travel in continental Europe. It was with considerable relief that I passed through passport control in October to visit my family in Spain, but I cannot guarantee I will not face trouble in future.

These are just some of the methods by which oppressive governments and powerful individuals can move outside their realms of influence to act against journalists and whistleblowers.

If democratic countries do not wake up to the public interest in this matter and defend us against these tactics, our societies will become more vulnerable to the spread of authoritarian influences from beyond our borders. ✖

Clare Rewcastle Brown is an investigative journalist focusing on environmental destruction in Malaysia and global financial corruption. She founded sarawakreport.org

50(04):28/29|DOI:10.1177/03064220211068684

ABOVE: The 46,000-year old Juukan Gorge rock shelters destroyed by mining giant Rio Tinto

Dream of saving sacred land dies in the dust

Australia's mining industry is at odds with the traditional beliefs of the Aboriginal population and, as **SCARLETT EVANS** reports, it is taking its toll on the country's indigenous heritage

MINING HOLDS A powerful sway over Australia. A staple part of its economic growth, the industry has expanded to make the country one of the world leaders in exports of coal, iron ore and a number of other minerals. Revenue brought in by the sector was estimated to be US$35.24 billion for the first quarter of 2021 alone.

But this prosperity has come at a price – and behind many mining sites lies the dislocation of indigenous people from their land and the destruction of artefacts sacred to its traditional owners.

Of particular note is Western Australia (WA), where mining contributes to almost half of gross value and where, says Tyronne Garstone, CEO of Kimberley Land Council, Aboriginal people make up between 3% and 4% of the population. "The greater interest is always going to be with the wider majority, and we've seen constant destruction happening throughout the state as a result," he said.

Over the last decade it would be easier to count which of the applications to exploit, develop and ultimately destroy more than 463 sites of indigenous significance have been denied than those that have not.

While many failed to attract high levels of media coverage or public awareness, this trend changed course with the destruction of the Juukan Gorge site in the Pilbara last year. The 46,000-year-old cave, containing artefacts including a 4,000-year-old plait

CREDIT: (left) PKKP/Rio Tinto; (inset) Paul Mayall Australia / Alamy

The scarring that happens in communities and the trauma it causes will go on for generations

of human hair made from the heads of numerous individuals, was destroyed by Anglo-Australian miner Rio Tinto in its quest for iron ore.

While by no means a one-off, it lent new fervency to the fight for indigenous land to be more adequately protected by law. A resulting inquiry into WA's Aboriginal Heritage Act was recently concluded, leading to a new bill being drawn up in the state legislature. But concerns have not yet been calmed. Calls are being made for the bill to be recalled amid claims that it still fails to give First Nation people due diligence.

Even outside the Heritage Act, the need to bring indigenous knowledge to bear in modern law remains important if we are to reconcile a contemporary legal structure with traditional understandings of land and its importance. While the renewed attention following Juukan Gorge gave some hope that change was on the horizon, disappointments around the new heritage bill show otherwise.

The fallout of Juukan Gorge

Findings from the Juukan Gorge inquiry were made public on 18 October 2021 after more than a year of public hearings. The report stated that Australia must do more to protect Aboriginal cultural heritage by overhauling what it termed "grossly inadequate" laws and called for the land's traditional owners to be given the right to withhold consent to the destruction of cultural heritage.

Inquiry chairman Warren Entsch told parliament: "It became apparent to the [joint standing] committee that the legislation designed to protect cultural heritage has in many, many cases directly contributed to the damage and destruction."

Exact details about the bill remained unknown until 19 November, the day before it was to be introduced to parliament.

Before this latest announcement, Garstone said that while the inquiry's findings were welcome, there was a

ABOVE: Patterson Bridge in South Kimberley, Western Australia, a region whose economy is dominated by mining

"concerning" lack of transparency around the latest version of the draft bill. He went on to caution that without true involvement of indigenous people in the entire decision-making process, "history will repeat itself".

Indeed, the bill has sparked backlash from indigenous groups and land councils, with particular ire over the lack of the right to review for traditional owners when it comes to deciding whether something can or cannot be destroyed.

"It's a devastating day for Aboriginal heritage," said Garstone. "We have repeatedly called on the [WA premier Mark] McGowan government to pause this bill and make the changes required to ensure Aboriginal heritage is protected. By ignoring our concerns, the McGowan government has treated Aboriginal people beneath contempt.

"Fundamentally, this bill will not protect Aboriginal cultural heritage and will continue a pattern of systematic structural racial discrimination against Aboriginal people."

Kimberley Land Council chair Anthony Watson said: "Aboriginal people are 'included' in the process only to be left without any influence over   →

→ the outcome. The Aboriginal Cultural Heritage Bill 2021 is whitewashing. Aboriginal concerns about Aboriginal heritage have been ignored. Once again, decisions about heritage will be made by non-Aboriginal people."

In response, the land council has written to the UN requesting the bill be withdrawn, with the group saying it will expose Aboriginal cultural heritage to "continued damage and destruction in violation of international human rights".

This path, Garstone says, has been well worn by First Nation people and the disappointment around this latest bill adds to the country's dark history – continuing to fail indigenous people

through their exclusion from law.

Many sites that have been subject to destruction of some kind have never received reparations, or even acknowledgement. The Kimberley region has experienced its own share of such tragedy, with the 2019 excavation of the Garnkiny or "moon dreaming" site, made famous by the artwork of senior traditional owner and artist Mabel Juli.

The black granite in the region is thought to make up the body of Goorlabal, a powerful Dreaming figure that takes the form of a serpent and is holder of law for the Gija people.

Exploration in the area was undertaken by Kimberley Granite Holdings, which removed parts of Goorlabal's tail and exported the rock to China without permission. Many Malarngowm people also had ancestors

buried on the land – and native title holder Rusty Peters (the brother of Mabel Juli) likened the act to "ripp[ing] my country open".

In October this year, the state government ruled that the miners who quarried and exported granite from this site would not be prosecuted – because the site was not registered under the 1972 Aboriginal Heritage Act until May 2020.

Such situations speak to the twofold tragedy that often happens – the initial destruction and the lack of prosecution of those who carried it out.

The role of traditional owners to protect sites of spiritual significance adds another layer of connection to land that Western frameworks neither understand nor account for.

"A senior man passed away after he found out the impact on the land," said

BELOW: The red earth scarred by mining is everywhere in Pilbara, Western Australia

CREDIT: Ian Waldie / Alamy Stock Photo

Garstone. "On his deathbed, he wanted people to know that it was the impact on his country which led to his passing and that he felt ashamed because it was his obligation in regard to maintaining and protecting that country, and he wasn't able to uphold that. This is something that Western society cannot appreciate – this type of sentiment that's coming from these people who have cultural obligations."

The intangible value of land

Indigenous voices are needed in the legislative process, not for political correctness but because much of the cultural and heritage significance of land is intangible – something that is not (and has never been) understood from a Westernised perspective of land and thus never accounted for in the Heritage Act.

By ignoring our concerns, the government has treated Aboriginal people beneath contempt

"It's very much a Western framework," said Garstone. "You've got old buildings, monuments etc that have been around for a while, and they've got heritage status – the significance that means you can't damage them. But this doesn't take into consideration the impact that certain places have, where

people have been telling stories for thousands of years and which afford a deep connection to Aboriginal people of who we are – and that's irreplaceable.

"Once we've lost something like that, we can't rebuild it. The scarring that happens in the communities and the trauma it causes will go on for generations."

Garstone makes clear that he believes genuine change can be enacted only through laws – and while this particular issue may be related to land, it is indicative of a wider failure to reconcile indigenous voices with modern law.

"We are heavily reliant on the laws to help us leverage our opportunities," he said. "This is something that should be taken into the broader context around the world about how indigenous people have been able to leverage their rights. It's never been through goodwill. It's always been through the court.

"We're not just talking about heritage when it comes to this issue. This is a broader story for us, looking at the suicide rates, incarceration rates, the unemployment rates... the entire lifecycle of Aboriginal people within Australia.

"This has broader ramifications. This is about land, but this should also open the doors for conversation around a broader holistic approach to how we get closer to unification."

While recent events around Juukan Gorge have given new hope that things might change, lawmakers are now trying to incorporate into legislation cultural issues that have been consistently marginalised.

Bringing traditional knowledge into decision-making is the first step towards rectifying this issue, but the road to reconciliation is a long one and will require increased and consistent efforts to share knowledge if it is to work. ✖

Scarlett Evans is a freelance journalist based in London, specialising in the mining industry and its environmental and social impacts

50(04):30/33|DOI:10.1177/03064220211068695

Bylines, deadlines and the firing line

It's not just pens and notebooks that journalists need in the USA, reports **RACHAEL JOLLEY**. It's sometimes gas masks and protective vests, too

JOURNALISTS ACROSS THE USA are increasingly in danger of physical attack as they cover the protests that are still raging in the toxic political atmosphere fomented by former president Donald Trump.

With protesters, police and spectators all carrying guns, reporting conditions can be as risky as those for war correspondents, according to one newspaper editor.

The idea that journalists are there to report demonstrations impartially is disappearing fast as protesters, from both the left and the right, turn on them, signalling that they believe the press is the enemy.

"We became conflict journalists in our own city," said Therese Bottomly, editor of The Oregonian, a daily newspaper in Portland, the biggest city in Oregon, which has been one of the

hotspots for protests – often ending in violence – throughout 2021.

"I think covering any event where weapons are openly displayed may require US journalists to think in ways we have not before about safety."

Portland's demonstrations have covered everything from Black Lives Matter to immigration to anti-vaccination rallies. They often involve confrontations between protesters and the police who, in some cases, have been supplemented by the National Guard. Buildings have been set on fire, with clouds of tear gas billowing around the city night after night as demonstrators meet lines of heavily armed law enforcement officers carrying AR-15 style weapons and munitions launchers.

Editors such as Bottomly have been forced to rethink their approach to staff safety. She said: "We initially were most

CREDIT: Nathan Howard / Stringer / Getty

LEFT: Another night, another protest in Portland. This time, on 12 April 2021, the murder of Daunte Wright, 20, led to conflict between police and demonstrators.

concerned about protection against tear gas-type agents so provided gas masks, goggles and the like. Several of our journalists were struck by police batons or police-fired munitions as they were trying to disperse protesters.

"We had safety conversations every night and the editor on duty repeatedly encouraged our journalists to put safety first, maintain awareness, have an exit strategy."

And she said The Oregonian's journalists did not have to cover stories where they feel unsafe.

"We purchased six ballistic vests to go with the helmets most of our journalists were already wearing," said Bottomly. "Several times we engaged outside security guards to accompany journalists and provide an extra set of eyes and ears to keep them safe."

For one protest near the state capital of Salem, the paper rented several motel rooms as a "safe harbour" for journalists.

While some might imagine that tension has decreased since the inauguration of Joe Biden as president, on the streets in key cities across the USA it remains high.

At the time of going to press, the US Press Freedom Tracker reported that of the 134 assaults on journalists it has documented in 2021, 105 of those are related to protests.

Journalists have had thousands of dollars-worth of equipment stolen. They have been kettled and restrained, beaten and chased down streets. They have also been tear-gassed by police but have also had to call the police to hold off crowds throwing things at them.

Index spoke to journalists in Washington, Los Angeles, Michigan and Portland about the violence they have been facing this year.

In July, photojournalist Eric Levai had $1,000-worth of equipment stolen

when masked people turned on him while he covered a transgender-rights protest in Los Angeles.

Levai, who works for the Daily Dot website as well as hosting a podcast, told the US Press Freedom Tracker website that he heard a shout before being charged and having his backpack containing a gas mask, goggles and a tripod snatched by seven or eight people.

"Protest coverage remains risky," Levai told Index, adding that he worries about wearing media ID while working. "Sometimes it's safer to wear it but sometimes not."

Reporter Joey Scott, who freelances in LA, is also wary of what can happen at protests, and he teams up with a friend for safety.

He told Index: "Despite the temporary restraining orders against police, they seem more than eager to harm protesters. [The police] will be investing in millions of dollars of training to better use less-lethal weapons and to infiltrate/surveil protesters. This will all most likely be used against the press in some way. They will also be changing tactics, though in what ways it is unclear, in terms of managing protests on the ground.

"When I feel there may be confrontation at a protest or rally, I pack my helmet and goggles. If I find it may be particularly confrontational, I pack my plate carrier [protective vest] to protect myself from any less-lethal rounds. I still feel unsafe out there at the moment.

"The adversarial relationship between the press and police still remains the same. That said, our state just passed a bill – SB98 – that allows the press to remain at a riot/protest/unlawful assembly without arrest. That has not been tested in the real world yet

and I imagine cops will find a way to invalidate who a member of the press is or find another excuse to arrest us. Lately, cops have been pointing their flashlights into cameras and being as confrontational as possible."

Marcin Wrona, a bureau chief in Washington, DC, for Polish TV channel TVN Discovery, has worked in the USA for many years. He said there had been significant changes in the past year.

"I can see that the hostile attitude towards the press is more and more obvious, or more visible; it's easier to get yourself in a difficult situation today than, let's say, a decade ago," he said.

Wrona's TV crew was attacked at a Black Lives Matter protest and had insults hurled at them during the attack on the Capitol on 6 January. In July, while covering a protest in Lafayette Square, Washington, the crowd turned on them and started to damage their equipment, throw things and threaten them, forcing them to abandon filming and flee the scene as demonstrators chased them. Police officers on bicycles came to their aid.

"Those three instances show me that people do not care what country you are from, what you are reporting about, how truthful you are, or whatever," said Wrona. "No, it's just enough to be a member of press to have a big target on your back."

He said the threats against journalists at protests were already affecting reporting. "When you have to watch your back all the time, and when you know that getting in the centre of developments may be dangerous, then you have to make a decision: 'OK, am I risking everything or not?' And of course, it influences reporting. I mean, there is no doubt about that." →

Covering events where weapons are openly displayed may require US journalists to think in new ways about safety

ABOVE: A photographer captured in direct confrontation with a protester in Washington DC on 6 January 2021, the day the US Capitol was stormed by supporters of Donald Trump

→ Part of the problem, he said, was that people were impersonating journalists by wearing press badges and media helmets, and that ramps up antagonism. "The word 'press' is now used not only by us."

Wrona, who has covered many protests including huge anti-war rallies during the George W Bush presidency, said the atmosphere towards the media had never been like it is today. He has now removed his address from his business cards and takes more safety precautions when preparing to cover a march or protest.

Some TV crews, although not his, are now working with security guards, which can affect reporting because it might deter people from talking to journalists.

He said the anger on the streets

mirrored some of the narratives in the media. "Some of the news outlets are kind of chasing their audience, which is becoming more and more polarised, and then the audience is watching only things that they agree with, but those things are polarising them even more."

Journalists working in small towns have also experienced changes. In August, Eric Baerren, a reporter in Mount Pleasant, Michigan, was covering a school board meeting about mask wearing. Afterwards, a parent asked him to remove photos from his camera. The parent tried to grab his phone and kick his camera out of his hand and police were called.

"It's a very difficult environment for journalists in this country right now." Baerren said.

The US Press Freedom Tracker has detailed other tactics used against journalists covering protests, including eggs being thrown and umbrellas being opened in front of TV crews and

photographers to impede their work. And journalist Alissa Azar was chased and beaten by a mob of the far-right group the Proud Boys in Olympia, Oregon.

Kirstin McCudden, managing editor of the US Press Freedom Tracker, said: "In Portland, there were more than 100 nights in a row of protests. And from that, we saw multiple journalists assaulted, arrested and equipment damaged multiple times."

These sorts of attacks have been recorded across the USA. She said the rise in incidents against reporters had happened as distrust in the media had risen. And while that distrust used to be embedded in only certain sections of society it is now widespread. "It's everybody," she said.

With the Pew Research Centre showing that trust in the media is at an all-time low, McCudden said "it follows that media is in the crosshairs time and again". ✖

Rachael Jolley is a contributing editor to Index and a research fellow at the Centre for the Freedom of the Media at Sheffield University.

50(04):34/36|DOI:10.1177/03064220211068696

Threats against journalists at protests are already affecting reporting

'a long overdue window'

MALIKA BOOKER

SONGS WE LEARN FROM TREES

AN ANTHOLOGY OF ETHIOPIAN AMHARIC POETRY

SONGS WE LEARN FROM TREES

Carcanet Classics

edited and translated by
CHRIS BECKETT
& ALEMU TEBEJE

*An Anthology
of Ethiopian
Amharic Poetry*

£18.99 / 978 1 78410 947 9 / CARCANET CLASSICS

CARCANET

Jennings

Our cartoonist turns his attention to medical information and disinformation

50(04):38/39|DOI:10.1177/03064220211068697

"I'VE DONE MY OWN RESEARCH"
BY BEN JENNINGS

BEN JENNINGS:
an award-winning
cartoonist for The
Guardian and The
Economist whose
work has been
exhibited around
the world

Maltese double cross

Four years on from Daphne Caruana Galizia's murder, lessons have not been learned. Justice for the investigative journalist's family remains elusive, writes **MANUEL DELIA**

MALTESE JOURNALIST DAPHNE Caruana Galizia was killed outside her home just before 3pm on 16 October 2017. She had spent that morning working at her dining room table next to her son Matthew. Less than half an hour before she was killed she posted her last article on her blog Running Commentary. She was commenting on evidence given in court by Keith Schembri, at the time Malta's prime minister's chief of staff and one of the most powerful people on the island.

Keith Schembri was testifying in a court case he brought against the then leader of opposition, Simon Busuttil. Busuttil was speaking at a protest march that gathered in Valletta after Caruana Galizia exposed Schembri's ownership of a secret company in Panama set up for him by Mossack Fonseca. Busuttil had branded Schembri "corrupt". Schembri did not like that.

"That crook Schembri was in court today, pleading that he is not a crook," wrote Caruana Galizia. "There are crooks everywhere you look now. The situation is desperate."

Two years later, in November 2019, Schembri was due to be cross-examined by Busuttil's lawyers in the same case. But by then a lot had changed. Criminal inquiries into Schembri's conduct had been opened. More evidence of wrongdoing had been published by journalists investigating the stories that killed Daphne. In court, Schembri refused to take the stand even under threat of jail. Instead, he chose to withdraw the complaint.

Within days Schembri was forced to resign. He was held by the police and interrogated in connection with Daphne's murder. He was released without charge but months later he was charged with some of the many cases of corruption Caruana Galizia had exposed him for. Schembri denies any wrongdoing; proceedings are ongoing.

There's some progress in the case against Caruana Galizia's alleged killers as well. So far, only one person has been convicted after admitting his role as an assassin and negotiating a reduced sentence in exchange for testifying for the prosecution. Two more assassins and three accessories to the crime await trial. A middleman has been pardoned and is also a witness for the prosecution. Also awaiting trial is Yorgen Fenech, the man charged with commissioning and paying for Caruana Galizia's murder.

Fenech is the scion of a local business family with fingers in many pies: hotels, casinos, property, and, since 2013, electricity. Fenech put together a consortium of local businesses with Siemens and the Azerbaijan state-owned gas company SOCAR. The consortium bid for a government contract to sell energy to the island for 18 years.

And they won the bid. The award was given on the advice of local firm Nexia BT. BT stands for Brian Tonna, the name of its owner and lead partner. In 2013, Tonna also owned and ran the Malta branch of Mossack Fonseca, the Panama law firm exposed by the Panama Papers.

At the same time that the selection board he advised awarded the energy contract to Fenech's firm, Tonna set up Panama companies for Schembri and Konrad Mizzi, then minister for energy. Tonna also set up a British Virgin Island company for one Cheng Chen, an Accenture consultant advising the Shanghai Electric Corporation that bought a chunk of the shares in Malta's state-owned energy company Enemalta. That deal was also sealed by Mizzi.

In a reply to an invitation to comment, Mizzi said "there is no connection whatsoever between my trust setup and Electrogas. Your allegation of impropriety is not backed up by any evidence whatsoever, and is thus defamatory. I do appreciate that your baseless allegation is part of a wider mudslinging strategy espoused by the political party in opposition, which you openly support, and as such I strongly reject it."

Tonna was also invited to comment but sent no reply. On several other occasions, Tonna has denied any wrongdoing.

Some time before she was killed Caruana Galizia discovered a company in Dubai called 17 Black. After her death journalists discovered a written brief from Nexia BT to Mossack Fonseca informing them that 17 Black, alongside another Dubai company called Macbridge, was the source of $2 million

It is certain that taxpayer money paid salaries of ministers and state officials that are, at least in part, responsible for Daphne's killing

to be paid every year to Schembri and Mizzi's Panama companies.

The owners of 17 Black and Macbridge have since been exposed. 17 Black belongs to Fenech. Macbridge belongs to Chen.

Mizzi, Schembri, and Fenech have so far faced no charges for corruption in the case that Caruana Galizia was investigating. It is now an element in the case for the prosecution of Fenech over Caruana Galizia's murder. Civil society activists complain that even by the notoriously slow standards of Malta's justice system this is hard to explain. The police are at pains to make it clear they have not shelved these investigations but five years since the Panama Papers and four since Caruana Galizia was killed, justice seems a long way away.

Schembri's former boss, Joseph Muscat, lost his job as prime minister six weeks after his right-hand man. He has had to answer questions by investigators particularly about his relationship with Fenech. Together with Schembri they shared a three-way WhatsApp group that discussed food and women when investigators had already briefed Muscat that Fenech was their prime suspect in a murder investigation.

The night before Fenech was apprehended by the coastguard trying to leave Malta aboard his yacht, Schembri spent hours on the phone with him. The calls were interrupted by middle of the night conversations between Muscat and Schembri.

Melvin Theuma, who admitted his involvement in the plot to kill Daphne and has been pardoned to turn state evidence, told the court that a member of Muscat's security detail offered payment to the alleged assassins to encourage them not to spill the beans. The same witness testified that the most powerful unelected official in the country, Schembri, gave him a government job when Fenech had hired him to recruit Daphne's killers. Theuma would get a monthly salary to do nothing. Schembri was invited to

ABOVE: Crowds call for the resignation of Joseph Muscat, then prime minister, after the arrest of a businessmen in the investigation of Daphne Caruana Galizia's murder

comment but did not reply. Previously, he has denied any wrongdoing.

It is certain that taxpayer money paid salaries of ministers and state officials that are, at least in part, responsible for Caruana Galizia's killing. An independent inquiry has found Malta's state partly responsible and has been particularly critical of Muscat's ministers who could have stopped Muscat when he decided to retain Schembri and Mizzi in office in spite of what Caruana Galizia and the Panama Papers had exposed their secret companies, set up right after they got to power in 2013.

The inquiry determined that impunity poisoned the atmosphere in Malta, and exposed Caruana Galizia to great risk. That risk, the isolation that she was left in, was exploited by her killers.

Malta's government today, led by Muscat's successor Robert Abela, claims things have changed. And yet, almost all of Abela's ministers served under Muscat and enabled Schembri and Mizzi. Abela himself was Muscat's lawyer. In his opposition to the public inquiry that found his ministers responsible for a murder, Abela had accused Daphne's

family of preferring to harm their country over justice for their mother. He has since apologised for the remark.

Malta is fast approaching a general election that will decide if the party and government under whose watch a journalist was killed is to be confirmed in power. By all accounts, Abela's re-election is a near certainty.

In spite of the continued impunity for the politicians and their associates, "fighting corruption" is very low in the list of priorities given by respondents to opinion polls. In this context anti-corruption journalism and activism calling for justice for a murdered journalist are met with hostility or indifference by much of the population. If Caruana Galizia's killing is to teach us anything, it is that that sort of indifference, hostility and isolation makes life for journalists very dangerous.

Four years after her killing, justice for Daphne Caruana Galizia remains elusive and the struggle for her family and their supporters remains uphill. And Malta's authorities keep looking for and finding ways of not learning the right lessons and making the right changes. ✖

Manul Delia is the author of Murder on the Malta Express

50(04):40/41|DOI:10.1177/03064220211068698

"Apple poisoned me: physically, mentally, spiritually"

Ashley Gjøvik, who was fired by the tech giant after blowing the whistle on toxic waste under her office, tells **MARTIN BRIGHT** that her fight will go on

ASHLEY GJØVIK KNEW things had become serious when she received an email on 9 September 2021 from Apple's Threat Assessment and Workplace Violence team asking her to discuss a "sensitive intellectual property matter".

Gjøvik, 35, had been raising concerns about toxic waste under her office for six months, and had become known as "The Apple Whistleblower", but this was the first time she had been contacted by this scary-sounding unit.

She emailed back to say she was "happy to help" but with one condition: everything had to be done via email. "I wanted everything in writing so they are not misrepresenting me, they're not trying to gaslight and intimidate me."

But she never discovered what the sensitive IP matter was because she was fired for failing to co-operate with the investigation, despite repeated attempts to express her willingness to do so. The letter terminating her employment accused her of disclosing "confidential product-related information" but did not go into detail.

By the time she was sacked, Gjøvik had become a fearsome employee-activist conducting a full-scale campaign over hazardous waste in Silicon Valley. She had gone public on workplace harassment, Apple's surveillance of employees and its culture of secrecy. But it all began when she started to raise perfectly regular concerns about her own safety and that of her fellow workers.

In February 2020, Gjøvik had moved into a new apartment in Santa Clara, California, only a short drive from her office in nearby Sunnyvale. On the face of it, Gjøvik had an enviable job as a senior engineering programme manager ("We work behind the scenes to make sure everything gets done. We make sure the products actually get out the door").

She worked hard in a stressful environment – while training to be a lawyer in her spare time – but prided herself on her resilience. Despite the punishing hours of work and study, she was in good health. However, within days of moving into the apartment, she started experiencing dizzy spells.

"I'm starting to have chest pain and palpitations and I'm like, what the hell is going on?" she told Index. She went to see about 20 different doctors and even attended a nervous system clinic at Stanford University. "My blood pressure's doing crazy stuff. My heart's doing crazy stuff, but no one knows why. I'm getting all these rashes. No one knows why. I have a growth on my thyroid… all this weird stuff happening all at once."

By the end of February, she was already so ill that she could barely function: "I'm passing out sitting. I can't focus. I have to lay down all the time. My body starts going nuts."

Before the pandemic hit, Gjøvik was already working from home and by March she was signed off on a medical leave of absence.

As the months passed and she became sicker and sicker, Gjøvik realised she was waking regularly at 3am feeling as if she was choking. She began to wonder if her failing health had anything to do with the apartment itself. By chance, one day in September 2020, she was talking to a friend whose husband was an engineer and he suggested she check the carbon monoxide levels.

She discovered a spike in volatile organic compounds (VOCs) in the early hours of the morning. These VOCs, essentially toxic gases, are present in everyday household products such as disinfectants, aerosols, pesticides and paints. But they are not usually found at levels dangerous to people's health. Nor do they tend to spike at particular times without a cause such as cooking or cleaning.

Gjøvik immediately set about doing some serious detective work. When she looked up the environmental assessment report on her apartment she saw it contained a 40-page section entitled "hazardous waste". Silicon Valley was favoured by defence contractors before it became the centre of America's tech miracle and was once dominated by factories and heavy industry.

It turned out the apartment was built on a so-called Superfund site, a designation from the US Environmental Protection Agency. Such sites demand a special industrial clean-up before people can live and work in the

> ≡ Apple was planning for the post-pandemic return to work, but Gjøvik felt it was unsafe

CREDIT: Handout

LEFT: "I had to get the word out," says Ashley Gjøvik, who became the 'Apple Whistleblower'

She raised her concerns with the California and Federal EPA as well the state and county departments of environmental health and the local water boards. She moved out of the apartment later that month and all the symptoms stopped immediately. She was even able to return to work.

By the spring of 2021, Gjøvik had become an armchair expert on Superfunds, vapour intrusion and the science of toxic groundwater plumes. So when she saw an email from Apple's environmental health and safety team on 17 March notifying staff of "a large-scale project" across the company's building portfolio to carry out vapour intrusion testing, alarm bells started ringing.

The building, a slick glass office with an octagonal atrium, had been leased by Apple since 2015 and was known to be built on the site of a factory owned by TRW Microwave Inc, a notorious Superfund polluter. Gjøvik found a 2016 report of vapour intrusion in homes next to the office and a 2019 lawsuit by the EPA against the polluters. The real concern was the presence of trichloroethylene (TCE), a carcinogen associated with kidney cancer.

Gjøvik was keen to know if the new testing was the result of a new vapour intrusion incident and asked if any testing had been carried out since Apple employees had moved in six years earlier. She was initially told not to discuss her concerns with anyone except her manager, the HR department and environmental health and safety so as not to cause panic.

But already Gjøvik was building a reputation as a toxic waste whistleblower through the campaign around her Santa Clara apartment. She had written an article in the local paper, San Francisco Bay View, entitled "I thought I was dying: My apartment was built on toxic waste". She had also brokered a meeting ➔

area, involving deep excavation and "backfilling" with concrete. If this is not carried out properly the risk is that vapour from toxic underground plumes can escape into the atmosphere (and people's homes).

Gjøvik discovered that so-called "vapour intrusion" can occur through sewer pipes, plumbing, sprinkler systems and air conditioning. She pestered her landlord and the fire department for diagrams of all the pipes in the building

to isolate the source. To this day she does not know exactly why the levels of toxic gas spiked at 3am, but she believes it is possible that it had something to do with the automated air conditioning or the flushing of the fire sprinklers.

"The apartment block had 1,800 units with two or three bedrooms. So, thousands of people could be sick and not know it. I literally could not sleep at night. I had to get the word out," said Gjøvik.

CREDIT: Hans Blossey / Alamy Stock Photo

→ with California Senate member Bob Wieckowsi to discuss her concerns.

In mid-April she visited experts in public health and occupational medicine at University of California San Francisco and it became increasingly clear that it would be difficult to separate her concerns about her former apartment from those about her office.

Throughout the spring and summer of 2021, Gjøvik put pressure on Apple to reveal why the new testing was being carried out and whether it was connected with cracks that had appeared in the floor of her office. She also urged her employers

My blood pressure's doing crazy stuff. My heart's doing crazy stuff, but no one knows why

to test the air in the office before the cracks were repaired to establish whether workers had been put at risk since 2015.

Apple was planning for the post-pandemic return to work, but Gjøvik said she felt it was unsafe for her and her colleagues to return to work without assurances about the toxic waste under their office. Some co-workers had been given special permission to return to work as early as May 2020.

The relationship with Apple had almost completely broken down by this point. The company did begin an investigation into Gjøvik's complaints of bullying and sexual harassment, but she believes this simply sparked further intimidation. In a last-ditch attempt to force Apple to engage publicly, she began live-tweeting her interactions with the company and eventually, in August, she was suspended on indefinite administrative leave.

In a statement on the case to the tech website The Verge, Apple spokesperson Josh Rosenstock said: "We are and have always been deeply committed to creating and maintaining a positive

ABOVE: The Apple HQ under construction in Cupertino, Silicon Valley, California, a place favoured by defence contractors before it became the centre of America's tech revolution

and inclusive workplace. We take all concerns seriously and we thoroughly investigate whenever a concern is raised and, out of respect for the privacy of any individuals involved, we do not discuss specific employee matters."

But Gjøvik is refusing to roll over: "I want to document it and show the world this is what Apple did: You poisoned me physically, mentally, spiritually. Fuck you guys."

Ashley Gjøvik has become a nightmare for Apple, which prides itself on its employees' loyalty. Following the classic whistleblower playbook, rather than address the issues she raised about toxic waste, the company has taken the decision to shoot the messenger. ✖

Martin Bright is editor of Index on Censorship

50(04):42/44|DOI:10.1177/03064220211068699

SPECIAL REPORT

"She turned city centres into theatres through her entrance into them, and the public became her audience, whether they were expecting it or not"

GOOD CHANCE THEATRE'S LITTLE AMAL WAS CREATED TO CELEBRATE HUMAN
MIGRATION AND CULTURAL DIVERSITIES | THE FIRST STEPS, PAGE 66

Keeping the flame alive as theatre goes dark

Theatre across the world is fighting new waves of repression, intolerance and nationalism, as well as financial cuts, at a time when a raging pandemic has threatened its existence. **NATASHA TRIPNEY** introduces our special report

FOR THE PAST two years, theatre has faced an existential crisis.

It is, after all, an artform that brings people together, that assembles audiences in rooms to share stories, an artform that often highlights structural inequality, corruption and injustice. It has the potential to be a powerful tool of resistance and solidarity. It has, therefore, often been viewed as a threat by oppressive regimes.

The pandemic temporarily put a stop to people's ability to congregate – theatres sat dark and empty for months. This enforced pause also granted governments licence to exert a greater degree of control over theatre artists and institutions. Theatre was now a public health threat and could, therefore, be more easily policed. But, as with so many consequences of Covid-19, the pandemic was merely working as an accelerant, exacerbating issues that already existed.

Efforts to exert control over theatre artists obviously predate Covid-19. Back in 2019, Viktor Orban's government's attempts to tighten its control over the performing arts in Hungary were met with protests and, in the same year, Freemuse reported more than 711 acts of violations of artistic freedom in 93 countries.

When the 2021 edition of Radar Ost, a festival of eastern European work at Berlin's Deutsches Theater opened in October, it did so under the overarching banner "Art[ists] at Risk". Its programme included work from Bosnia and Herzegovina, Russia, Ukraine and Belarus and consisted of companies subject to oppression in their respective countries – but it was striking how widely that label could be applied.

The climate for artists in Belarus has deteriorated dramatically since the widely disputed elections in August 2020. Alyaksandr Lukashenka has brutally cracked down on all opposition and, in December 2021, a decade after its co-founding artistic directors Natalia Kaliada and her husband Nicolai Khalezin first sought political asylum in the UK, Belarus Free Theatre was forced to move its entire ensemble out of the country.

This huge decision, to uproot the 16-strong company and their families, reflects the level of risk of reprisals they faced in Belarus today. Kaliada and Khalezin have been subjected to death threats and, as opponents of the regime, the company found themselves in an increasingly untenable and unsafe position.

The fall of Afghanistan and the resurgence of the Taliban has also placed artists in jeopardy, displacing many from their country. The period has also seen the increase in nationalist cultural policies in numerous countries, as well as increasing government intrusion into artistic decision-making processes and artistic leaderships.

There is increasing intolerance to work which challenges or interrogates the dominant narrative. In Serbia, for example, Zlatko Pavković's production Srebrenica. When We, the Killed, Rise Up was the subject of protests, as was the Miredita, dobar dan festival, an event which brings Kosovar and Serbian artists together.

The pandemic has also left theatre artists financially vulnerable and exposed their already precarious position. In countries without healthy state subsidies, this was particularly evident. Funding for the arts has been cut in many countries, with theatre at best treated as an afterthought, at worst a containment. In many countries recovery packages

OPPOSITE: (top) The aftermath of the destruction of Albania's National Theatre in Tirana by government forces on 17 May 2020 and (bottom) the beautiful theatre, built by the Italians in 1938, which protesters failed to save

were inadequate if they existed at all. In Albania, in a symbolically potent gesture, the country's National Theatre was razed, an act carried out in darkness and during lockdown when it was hard for people to protest.

In the UK, rights are being gradually eroded and pressure was placed on arts organisations to publicly express their gratitude when the recipients of the Culture Recovery Fund were eventually announced.

But this hasn't stopped people making theatre. Far from it. Even in the bleakest moments over the last two years, when it was uncertain when – or even if – theatres would reopen, artists found ways to make and share work, to adapt and evolve.

At a time when countries were turning inwards, digital innovations allowed audiences around the world to watch each other's work, to immerse themselves in other cultures, to cross borders even while travel was prohibited. The journey of the puppet Little Amal across Europe has created a symbol of solidarity and empathy with migrants at a time when governments are hardening their stance on immigration.

Theatre invites its audience to see the world through the eyes of others – something which feels more important than ever. ✖

Natasha Tripney is reviews editor of The Stage

50(04):46/47|DOI:10.1177/03064220211068700

There is increasing intolerance to work which challenges or interrogates the dominant narrative

Testament to the power of theatre as rebellion

The Belarus Free Theatre, whose 16 members have now gone into exile to escape the Lukashenka regime, are preparing to perform at the Barbican in London in 2022. **KATE MALTBY** joins a rehearsal

N A SKYSCRAPER in the heart of the City of London, a surprisingly airy rehearsal space hosts a group of Europe's boldest theatre-makers.

In the centre of the room, a woman trudges in a circle with the juddering, formal rhythms of a fatigued sergeant-major, a vacuum-cleaner held out before her like a rifle. On the other side of the "stage", an actor playing a surgeon is operating on a seemingly conscious patient.

Two stage-managers watch from the front: behind an otherwise conventional rehearsal table littered with sound equipment and notes, someone has hung the white-and-red flag, or *byel-chyrvona-byely s'tsyah*, which has become the emblem of Belarusian resistance to the dictator Alyaksandr Lukashenka.

> We went on to the streets, performing to the crowds of protesters, and they were performing back in the form of their protest

I spot a souvenir water-bottle from the Human Rights Foundation's Oslo Freedom Forum. On a small chair at the side of the room, a voice issues from a Zoom video running on a laptop. This is Nikolai Khalezin, founder with his wife Natalia Koliada of the Belarus Free Theatre company, directing a rehearsal over video link.

Today Khalezin is leading his company by Zoom because he seems to have a cold – and, in the time of Covid, no one can be too careful. But unlike most directors working in London, he has long practised in making theatre remotely. Since 2011, Khalezin and Koliada have held political asylum in the UK, a necessity for survival in the face of repeated harassment and imprisonment at the hands of Lukashenka's regime.

Khalezin was a journalist before he became a theatre-maker, working for three independent Belarusian newspapers successively closed as the autocracy tightened its grip. But in all the years in the UK, Khalezin and Koliada have never stopped co-ordinating their theatre company, keeping in close but covert contact with artists on the frontline of Belarusian resistance, who have risked their freedom and even their lives to perform "unregistered" theatre in garages and private homes around their homeland.

Long before the pandemic, directing his actors by video-link had become Khalezin's norm. Now, given the

ABOVE: A rehearsal in London for the Dogs of Europe, a psychological drama set in the near future, scheduled for its premiere in March 2022

vicious repression which followed Lukashenka's attempt to assert himself in August 2020 as the "winner" of a sixth term as president, the rest of the 16-member Belarus Free Theatre, and their families, have fled their native land to reunite in London.

Ostensibly, the artists of the Belarus Free Theatre are now refugees. "What can foundations and activists in the West specifically do to help?" I ask Khalezin, perhaps naively.

"What can you do to help? Imagine 20 people arriving in a new country without a roof, without spare clothes, with nowhere to go – then it becomes quite easy to picture what you can do to help."

But they are also rehearsing in

London as prestigious invited artists, programmed to premiere their latest production at the Barbican Centre in March 2022. Dogs of Europe, first performed in an early version in Minsk in 2019 – crowds of supporters turned up in spite of the fear of arrest – is an adaptation of Alhierd Bacharevic's mammoth novel set in a dystopic Europe of 2049.

In the book, most of Asia has fallen under a secret-service dominated Russian "reich", while an ever more fragmented western Europe grapples with a refugee crisis. The title seems to recall W H Auden's poem on the death of Yeats: "In the nightmare of the dark / All the dogs of Europe bark / And the living nations wait / Each sequestered in its hate."

The novel was published in 2017, but as a long-term collaborator of Bacharevic, Khalezin first saw a version in 2014 – since then, he says, "it has

become closer to our contemporary world even quicker than I had imagined." He is still working on condensing Bacharevic's 900 pages into a 150 minute show and on scaling up his company's flexible rehearsal versions to fit the Barbican Theatre's 1,162-seat main space.

Not that the Belarus Free Theatre's audiences have ever been small. Part of the problem of performing for years in secret scratch locations around Minsk has always been the sheer number of people who regularly turn up, hungry for intellectual immediacy. The level of direct intervention by Lukashenka's thugs has varied on and off – part of any surveillance state's strategy is always to fuel uncertainty and surprise – but in 2007, for example, the entire company were arrested in the middle of a performance of Edward Bond's Eleven Vests.

Ironically, Bond's play for young people explores the abuse of liberty by state institutions, both school and army – the arrests came within three weeks of a summit on political liberty in eastern Europe at which Vaclav Havel had hosted the Belarus Free Theatre at his country home in the Czech Republic.

With the eruption of protests in 2020, however, the theatre company found themselves performing on open streets. "Minsk is full of courtyards," says Svetlana Sugako, the company's general manager. "We went on to the streets, and so did everybody else, so there we were, performing to the crowds of protesters, and they were performing back in the form of their protest."

Sugako discovered the Belarus Free Theatre in 2007, after being taken by a friend to a bar and rolling her eyes at the mere concept of theatre. "I had only seen the official, patriotic stuff – the state produces these long shows of official history and calls it theatre."

Inside, the company were performing their internationally acclaimed version of Sarah Kane's 4.48 Psychosis. "It was about suicide, and psychosis, and pain – and the government doesn't allow us to have plays which show this, because we are supposed to be a perfect society, so officially we don't have suicide, we don't have psychosis, we don't have pain. And it was right up in my face, performed at the bar, just like I'm talking to you now."

Sugako immediately got involved. Shortly afterwards she was arrested with the group, and when I look at →

ABOVE: Nicolai Khalezin directs rehearsals in a skyscraper in the City of London

It is hell. There are no human rights outside prison. So imagine what happens inside.

→ accounts of her imprisonment she has given elsewhere, I read harrowing stories about being humiliated while naked, and forced to listen to male prisoners being raped with objects in the next room. So I don't press her. But she alludes to that particular stint in prison later in our conversation, when she talks about the experiences of being detained again last year in the aftermath of Lukashenka's crushing of the courtyard protests.

"It was bad before. But even compared to that first time, now it is hell. There are no human rights outside prison. So imagine what happens inside."

There are still more than 600 political prisoners in Belarus

BELOW: Nicolai Khalezin and Natalia Kaliada, co-founding artistic directors of BFT

(Lukashenka, in a recent interview with the BBC, called them "criminals".) The Belarus Free Theatre have been working with Index on Censorship to smuggle letters from prison and publish them on the Index website as Letters from Lukashenka's Prisoners.

What feels frustrating, observing the Belarus Free Theatre's development, is how many times it seems to have dropped from the Western radar over the past few years. Ten years ago, they were a liberal cause célèbre – I first encountered their work at an event at the Young Vic in London hosted by Index on Censorship in 2010, which seemed to have every progressive theatre luminary in attendance.

Many friends have stood firm, including the actor Samuel West and the playwright Sir Tom Stoppard, who also has a long-standing relationship with Index. But often, attention seems to flicker fashionably. Khalezin attributes this in part to the sheer wave of people in crisis globally: "You have people in need from Afghanistan, you have people from Syria – we shouldn't be competing with each other for help, but our stories should all be reason to look beyond your borders, to build more bridges."

Most of the company – all of whom

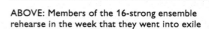

ABOVE: Members of the 16-strong ensemble rehearse in the week that they went into exile

have hair-raising tales about escaping Belarus – are likely to be based in Poland for the foreseeable future, partly because living in London is more expensive.

Conversely, the infectiously hopeful aspect of the Belarus Free Theatre is its unfettered advertisement for the power of theatre as rebellion. Critical conversations about art as freedom of expression inevitably revolve around the naysayers' question: "yes, but does it actually change anything?"

For 15 years, Khalezin and Koliada have been bringing people together in a nation whose government goes to extreme lengths to keep people apart. Theatre is shared experience – this much we know – and one of the markers of Lukashenka's regime is his attempt to deny citizens shared experience.

In October 2020, during the height of the election protests, people were forbidden from gathering in public places in groups of more than three and private gatherings were banned outright. (This supposedly was a health measure – but, as Sugako observes, "Belarus has no coronavirus. Officially. We are a perfect country, remember?").

Whether gathering people in private spaces, or engaging inquiring minds at a public protest, the Belarus Free Theatre brings people together. And when people come together, things begin to happen. ✖

Kate Maltby is deputy chair of trustees at Index on Censorship

50(04):48/50|DOI:10.1177/03064220211068701

PICTURED: Index asked Reza Shirmarz – shown at a theatre in Athens – to respond to Beckett's play

My dramatic tribute to Samuel Beckett and Catastrophe

More than three decades after Index published the celebrated playwright's work dedicated to the Czech dissident Vaclav Havel, censored Iranian writer Reza Shirmarz has responded with his own play, Muzzled. He talks to **MARK FRARY**

N 1982, SAMUEL Beckett wrote the short play Catastrophe about control and censorship and dedicated it to the Czech dramatist Vaclav Havel who at the time was languishing in prison for daring to challenge the authorities with his work.

When Havel was finally released, he wrote his own play, Mistake, as a response to the one Beckett had written in solidarity.

In February 1984, in one of the most significant milestones in the history of Index on Censorship, both plays were published for the first time (you can see these in our archive at **tinyurl.com/catastropheplay** and **tinyurl.com/mistakeplay**)

Now, in the year that Index celebrates its 50th birthday, we asked Iranian playwright Reza Shirmarz to write his own response to Beckett's Catastrophe.

Shirmarz was born in Tehran in 1974 and raised in an educated, multicultural (Persian, Turkish, Russian and Kurdish) family surrounded by books on literature, philosophy and history.

"When I was a teen, I grew fond of drama, theatre and music and began to read the world's dramatic texts more meticulously from the Greeks to the contemporary playwrights as well as translate the ones I liked," Shirmarz told Index.

As part of his education in theatre, Shirmarz studied the works of many of the theatre world's greats, including Beckett.

"Beckett is an architect of silence," he said. "He uses silence to give a harmonious interpretation of the words he builds his post-dramatic situations upon. This interaction between silence and words under the strong shadow of constant karmic repetition of lexical structures, sounds, silences, etc. gives the playwright a great chance to create innovative moments through which he gives his interpretation of the status quo."

Shirmarz began writing his own poems and plays and soon received accolades for his trilogy Cinnamon Stars, Crystal Vines and The Lanterns

If you are not an advocate of the ayatollahs' devious unscrupulous ways, you are an outsider, an outlaw

are Weeping which documented three decades of sociopolitical life in Iran.

Despite the praise from audiences and critics, Shirmarz gained unwanted attention from elsewhere.

"The plays were censored or banned by the fundamentalists when I tried to stage them or when they were sold out and the major publishing companies in Iran attempted to republish them," he said.

"Any sort of social criticism is the red line for the regime of Ayatollahs. My plays are all against the status quo in Iran and reveal the fact that morality can be unethical in countries under religio-ideological regimes, that religion and ideology together can change into an uncontrollably ferocious monster which tends to devour the entire society including itself, that the revolutions based on religious wiles and ideological lies go through a devastating process of political cannibalism as well as self-cannibalism."

Shirmarz eventually chose to emigrate to Greece because of Iran's "extremely corrupt system which chooses to support its proponents and excommunicate its opponents at any price".

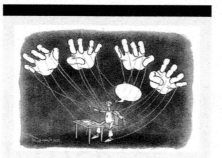

Kianoush Ramezani, 48, who has drawn our cartoon (overleaf), fled Iran in a crackdown after the 2009 election

He told Index: "If you are not an advocate of their devious unscrupulous ways, you are an outsider, an outlaw, and you need to move out if you want to survive, but if you are or play the role of the devil's advocate, they will return the favour, let you work under strict censorship, or they may even promote you a national celebrity."

As a censored writer himself, what are Shirmarz's views on Beckett's Catastrophe?

"Catastrophe is about censored communication, the ritualistic representation and the symbolic image of human relationship constrained by external forces, a deterministic, political and post-dramatic text which demonstrates how humans are coerced to be and live in a torturous limbo."

"[In Catastrophe] Beckett's Protagonist is deprived of free will by the systems surrounding him and the systematic control imposed by others, except at the moment he moves his head up and looks at the spectators.

"Despite his psychosomatic pain, he talks through his silence and protests through his immobility. As so-called social actors and audiences, we are reminded by the playwright that we are not able to get out of the cage the sociopolitical conventions have imprisoned us in and we must abide by the unbreachable laws brought in by the global structures and conglomerates in order to survive."

Muzzled, Shirmarz's response to Catastrophe, is published here in Index for the first time. ✖

Mark Frary is associate editor at Index on Censorship

50(04):51/59|DOI:10.1177/03064220211068702

Muzzled

A play by REZA SHIRMARZ

Dramatis personae
ACTRESS
COSTUME DESIGNER
DIRECTOR
PLAYWRIGHT
STAGE MANAGER
TWO MEN

(Shrill whistles are blown in the darkness. PLAYWRIGHT and ACTRESS appear gradually, sitting back to each other on the bed at the centre. ACTRESS's fragile red undies are visible underneath her casual transparent dress. She is pregnant, but she is at an early stage and her belly has expanded a bit. He is wearing white underwear.)

PLAYWRIGHT: They're coming.

ACTRESS: *(taking a bite of a banana)* How do you know?

PLAYWRIGHT: An old friend informed me.

ACTRESS: Twenty-four months ...

PLAYWRIGHT: *(angrily kidding)* Two years in that shithole isn't long enough to burn us out, is it?

ACTRESS: *(feels a bit on edge)* I promise, even if they force you to spend more time in jail, I won't be down in the dumps ... *(dubious)* ever. I know though they don't want us only to feel down, they want us, they want everybody, to be paralysed with fear.

PLAYWRIGHT: Yeah, they're totally afraid of people shattering the silence. That'd be their end. (Pause. Emphasising the positive.) They might let me out on parole after serving a couple of months. Who knows?

ACTRESS: Hopefully, darling. *(standing up)* Red or white?

PLAYWRIGHT: Red, as always. *(Walking with a bit of hip motion and body circles and waves and*

trying to capture his attention, she leaves the stage and disappears into the darkness) I'm going to write more plays if they let me, sweetheart. You know what's going on there.

ACTRESS: *(from the backstage)* I'll be waiting to devour them. I can't get enough of it. (Short pause.) How much time we've got?

PLAYWRIGHT: Not much. The bastards are on their way... could be here any moment.

ACTRESS: *(rushes back with two glasses of red wine)* I can't believe they're taking you away from me ... that you should spend two years ... *(hands him the glass and kisses his forehead)* that's unfair. Locked up just for writing a couple of plays? *(takes a sip and sits on his knees)* Murderers, bribers, fraudsters, rapists, muggers, and smugglers are out there living their filthy lives freely disguised themselves as politicians, men of God and businessmen, while people like you ...

PLAYWRIGHT: *(hugs her from behind and kisses her on the neck)* Don't worry, darling. I promise I'm going to get back to you ASAP. *(Jokingly)* I'm going to be a good boy. Won't give them a chance to torture me and hurt me, not for me, only for you and *(touches her stomach)* her.

ACTRESS: *(takes his hand and kisses it)* She's going to be the only connection between us... *(Stands up and walks away)* the only hope.

Pause.

PLAYWRIGHT: *(puts the glass on the bedside table and falls back on the bed)* I've been having the same nightmare most nights, since they've banned my plays and threatened my producers, my crew, my friends, my family... I saw myself chained →

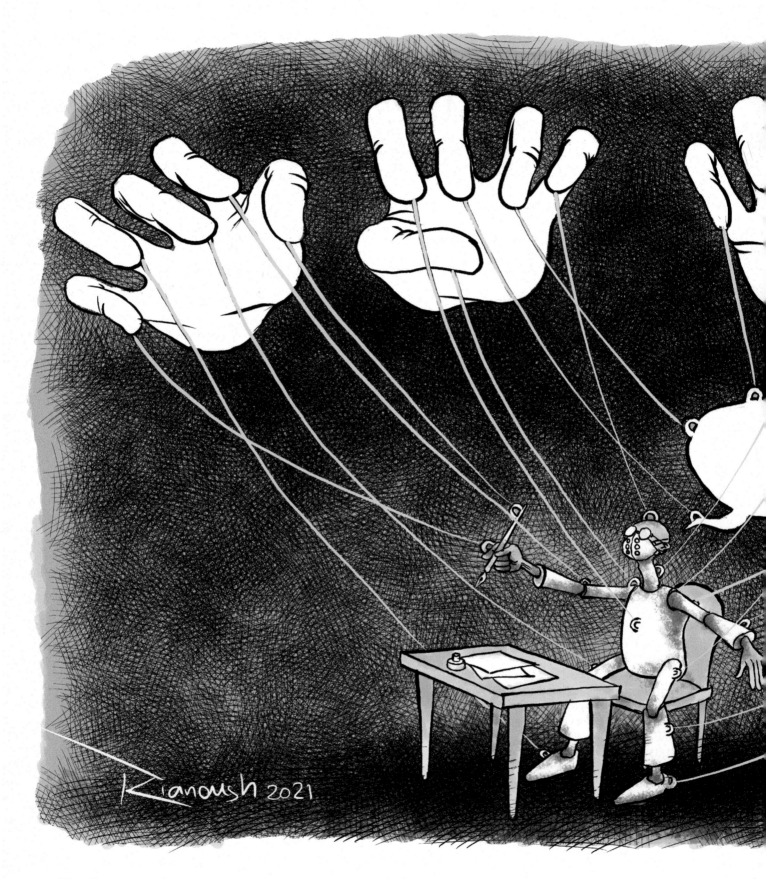

→ by each wrist, I'm pulled apart and my body is about to be torn into two pieces. I struggle to get rid of the chains. The more movements I make, the more I'm pulled apart. I can see the blood gushing from the cracks of my chest and belly. I struggle to shout wildly and furiously… but they've muzzled me. *(After a short pause)* Eventually, the chains change into strings and two monstrous puppeteers take control of my limbs. They move my head, my hands, and my feet. They have control over all my actions and thoughts. They even speak for me. They move my lips and say the things I never meant. Then, their voice changes into whistles. They whistle so loudly that I can't take it anymore, I try to get rid of the strings, but the more movements I make, the more they take me under control.

(Whistles are blown. Upstage left two men come into sight. Wearing white gloves, their heads and chests are not visible. A general wash of light illuminates the stage. DIRECTOR and COSTUME DESIGNER rush in. STAGE MANAGER receives a long sheet of paper, evidently a list, from the men and hastily approaches DIRECTOR.)

DIRECTOR: Again? Fucking bastards!
MANAGER: *(as reading)* "No bed is permitted on the stage. The bed must be replaced by two chairs at least a metre apart. One on the left, the other one on the right."
DIRECTOR: *(to MANAGER)* A sofa is a better option. Isn't it? →

We say yes to their stupid choices and we are going to dance to their tune for the rest of our life

CREDIT: Kianoush Ramezani

→ MANAGER: We know that the main issue is that they should not appear to touch, not the bed or sofa.

DIRECTOR: We say yes to their stupid choices and we are going to dance to their tune for the rest of our life. You understand? Sofa. Write it down! *(MANAGER writes it down)* Next.

MANAGER: *(as reading)* They say that their upper and lower body must be fully covered. "Sexually explicit," that's what they call it.

DIRECTOR: *(to COSTUME DESIGNER)* Isn't this obnoxious?

DESIGNER: Yes, but…

MANAGER: *(as reading)* They believe "even partial nudity is against our beliefs".

DIRECTOR: Yeah, I know… the forbidden fruit, which sometimes tastes the sweetest.

MANAGER: They won't let us go public with the underwear.

DIRECTOR: Anyway, there's no time for flippancy here. *(To Costume Designer)* What do you think?

DESIGNER: We've got red stretch leggings and a cream ribbed cardigan for her … black jeans and a blue close-fitting T-shirt for him *(exits immediately)*.

MANAGER: But it's written here *(reads it out loud)* "baggy pants and shirts". That's what they want from us.

DIRECTOR: I don't give a shit what they want. I won't let them ruin what we've worked for like dogs. This is art here, man. It's totally over their head and their suggestion is ridiculous. It won't work at all. The audience has to see her belly to notice that she's pregnant. Her body is paramount here, cannot be covered in the shitty baggy thing…

(MANAGER writes it down. COSTUME

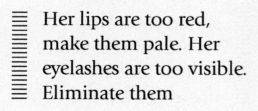

Her lips are too red, make them pale. Her eyelashes are too visible. Eliminate them

DESIGNER rushes back with the outfits and helps PLAYWRIGHT and ACTRESS put them on, but STAGE MANAGER tries to stop him from putting the outfits on her.)

MANAGER: We need to take care of her "curves" first.

DESIGNER: Good God! They'd stopped caring about female body curves.

MANAGER: *(Shows him)* Here, take a look. *(reading)* "body curves including breasts, hips, butts and thighs must be eliminated. Female's hair must be fully covered. Keep her hair straight under the scarf."

DIRECTOR: *(approaching them)* What's going on?

DESIGNER: *(rushes out again)* We need cincher belts and a scarf.

DIRECTOR: Cinchers for a pregnant woman? Isn't this moronic?

ACTRESS: It'll make me feel as though I'm suffocating. Isn't this barbaric?

DIRECTOR: They won't stop until they asphyxiate us all one day.

MANAGER: *(reading from the list)* "She must wear a thick scarf and the hair style should not be discernible under the scarf. Her make-up is too visible. Her lips are too red, make them pale. Her eyelashes are too visible. Eliminate them."

(COSTUME DESIGNER rushes in with cinchers and a scarf and starts putting them on ACTRESS flattening her curves and covering her hair.)

DIRECTOR: Next.

MANAGER: Apple instead of banana. *(reads)* "It is forbidden for women to eat banana or similar fruits on the stage. It sounds inappropriate. Apple is a better choice."

DIRECTOR: *(furious)* It is only a banana. She needs it. She's got a baby on the way and she needs to eat some goddamn sugary fruits. What is the fucking problem with the banana?

MANAGER: They say *(reads again)* "it sounds inappropriate."

DIRECTOR: *(bawls)* That's not my grandfather's

cock. *(After a short pause)* Well, then give her instead *(winks angrily at ACTRESS giving her a quick wry smile)* a thick "cucumber" to eat. That's going to cheer the dirty-minded assholes up.

MANAGER: It might be equally "inappropriate." *(to the audience while other characters remain motionless)* He has recently come back from abroad where he used to work freely. He doesn't know yet what's going on here. He has no idea what he's going to go through if he violates the rules, if he refuses to uphold the religious values, if he ignores the political norms, if he breaks the traditional laws, if he doesn't care about the "suggestions" of the authorities, if he continues to defy the "orders" *(everybody moves again).*

DIRECTOR: I won't make it an apple, I won't give them what they want. This is my fucking stage… My stage, my rules. You understand? Next.

MANAGER: *(reads from the list)* "Shithole" needs to change into "penitentiary."

DIRECTOR: Prison or jail? *(to PLAYWRIGHT)* What do you think?

PLAYWRIGHT: *(showing his jeans and T-shirt)* I'm a hundred and fifty percent with you on that. "Penitentiary" is for serious crimes, better to use "prison" or "jail" where prisoners are kept temporarily.

DIRECTOR: *(Takes a glance at MANAGER)* I agree. Put it down. "Prison" instead of "shithole." *(MANAGER jots it down)* Next.

MANAGER: *(reading)* "The dialogue – I know though they don't want us only to feel down, they want us, they want everybody, to be paralysed with fear – must change into – I know though they don't want us only to feel down, they want us and all wrongdoers to be punished and be full of remorse for their sins."

DIRECTOR: You serious? *(incandescent with rage)* Is this a fucking joke?

PLAYWRIGHT: This is going to ruin the whole notion behind the dialogue. This is absurd.

MANAGER: We need to stick to the guidelines if we want our play to get permission, if we want to continue our profession.

DIRECTOR: *(to MANAGER)* Come on, don't be such a coward, grow some fucking balls. *(to*

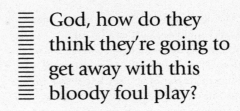

God, how do they think they're going to get away with this bloody foul play?

PLAYWRIGHT) Let's think of something. Just be quick about it…

PLAYWRIGHT: We could say "I know though they don't want us only to feel down, they want us, they want everybody, to feel… *(cannot find the proper word)* to feel… eh… safe." How about that?

DIRECTOR: You're not serious. That's far from what the original words meant, *(after a short pause)* but what else could we do? We're running out of time. Let's move on. *(To MANAGER)* Next.

MANAGER: They've suggested "Coca-Cola or Fanta" instead of "red or white wine".

PLAYWRIGHT: *(ironically)* How about citrus peach cooler and pomegranate mojito mocktail?

DIRECTOR: *(To MANAGER)* Absolutely not. Nothing less than beer or cider, I'm telling you. *(To himself)* God, how do they think they're going to get away with this bloody foul play?

MANAGER: We know that "Coca-Cola or Fanta" are the only choices we have, but anyways… *(Jotting it down and reading concurrently)* "Words like darling and sweetheart must be crossed out."

PLAYWRIGHT: Perhaps *(addressing ACTRESS who is clearly almost suffocating in the cincher belts)* "my dearest" or "honey" are better synonyms, aren't they, love?

DIRECTOR: *(stops MANAGER who wants to say something)* Shut up and jot it down, "my dearest" and "honey."

(MANAGER jots it down reluctantly. Now COSTUME DESIGNER puts the red stretch leggings and a cream ribbed cardigan on ACTRESS.)

ACTRESS: *(letting out strangulated whimpers)* I →

→ can't fucking breathe. How can I move around, act and talk? And I'm as flat as a board.

DIRECTOR: *(to the audience while others remain motionless)* They're creating a maze for us we never going to get out of it. They know how to neutralise our creativity, our endeavours, our fucking presence. But it is what it is. They don't want us to have a real say about what we're doing here, do they? *(smiles bitterly)* Or we might think a different line of work in the future *(everybody moves again)*.

ACTRESS: *(strives to get used to the cinchers)* I've never done this. *(tumbles into the arms of PLAYWRIGHT)*

PLAYWRIGHT: *(jokingly)* You're a newcomer, darling. You're going to get used to it. Think about your future career. This is just the first step.

(PLAYWRIGHT and COSTUME DESIGNER help ACTRESS walk around and get used to it as she might tumble any moment.)

MANAGER: *(reading)* "Kisses, hugs, or any sort of touch must be omitted from the play and its performance."

DIRECTOR: *(now sits down feeling exhausted and light and drags on a cigarette leaning on the wall)* Next.

MANAGER: *(reading faster and louder as he goes on)* "Instead of the word – bastards – used to describe the police, it is necessary to use the law enforcement officers."

DIRECTOR: *(pulls on the cigarette)* Next.

MANAGER: "The word, devour, and the sentence – I can't get enough of it – are lascivious. Cross them out."

DIRECTOR: Next.

MANAGER: "The sentence – Murderers, bribers, fraudsters, rapists, muggers, and smugglers are out there living their filthy lives freely disguised themselves as politicians, men of God and businessmen, while people like you … – needs to change into – Murderers, bribers, fraudsters, rapists, muggers, and smugglers also spend time serving. They must be punished in order not to turn to crime again."

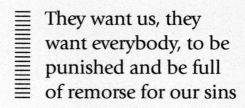

They want us, they want everybody, to be punished and be full of remorse for our sins

DIRECTOR: Next.

MANAGER: "The sentence – they've banned my plays and threatened my producers, my crew, my friends, my family… – must be crossed out."

DIRECTOR: Next.

MANAGER: "The sentence – they're totally afraid of people shattering the silence. That'd be their end – must change into – They're only afraid of God. That strengthens their faith and it's the beginning of their journey."

DIRECTOR: *(draws on the cigarette)* Next.

(Dead Blackout. Shrill whistles are blown. After a while PLAYWRIGHT and ACTRESS gradually become visible sitting next to each other on a sofa located at the centre. ACTRESS's body seems flat in the red stretch leggings and a cream ribbed cardigan and there are no body curves visible. No expanded belly. PLAYWRIGHT in his black jeans and a blue close-fitting T-shirt tries to stay physically distant from ACTRESS.)

PLAYWRIGHT: They're coming.

ACTRESS: *(taking a bite of a huge cucumber)* How do you know?

PLAYWRIGHT: An old friend informed me.

ACTRESS: Twenty-four months…

PLAYWRIGHT: *(angrily kidding)* Two years in that "prison" isn't long enough to burn us out, is it?

ACTRESS: *(feels a bit on edge)* I promise, even if they force you to spend more time in jail, I won't be down in the dumps… *(dubious)* ever. "I know though they don't want us only to feel down, they want us, they want everybody, to be punished and be full of remorse for our sins."

PLAYWRIGHT: Yeah, "they're only afraid of God.

That strengthens their faith and it's the beginning of their journey." (Pause. Emphasising the positive.) They might let me out on parole after serving a couple of months. Who knows?

ACTRESS: Hopefully, "honey". *(standing up carefully)* "Beer or cider?"

PLAYWRIGHT: "Beer" as always. *(Walking without any feminine waves and circles, she leaves the stage and disappears into the darkness)* I'm going to write more plays if they let me, my dearest. You know what's going on there.

ACTRESS: *(from the backstage)* I'll be waiting to "read" them. You know that I've got a soft spot for them. (Short pause.) How much time we've got?

PLAYWRIGHT: Not much. "The law enforcement officers" are on their way… could be here any moment.

ACTRESS: *(comes back with two glasses of beer, trying not to tumble)* I can't believe they're taking you away from me… that you should spend two years… *(hands him the glass and sends him a kiss from distant)* that's unfair. Locked up just for writing a couple of plays? (takes a sip and sits on the sofa next to him trying to avoid any physical contact) "Murderers, bribers, fraudsters, rapists, muggers, and smugglers also spend time serving. They must be punished in order not to turn to crime again."

PLAYWRIGHT: *(sends her a kiss)* Don't worry, darling. I promise I'm going to get back to you ASAP. *(Jokingly)* I'm going to be a good boy. *(jumps and kneels in front of her)* Won't give them a chance to torture me and hurt me, not for me, only for you and *(points to her flat belly without touching it)* her.

ACTRESS: *(also points to her own belly)* She's going to be the only connection between us…

≡ Eventually, the chains change into strings and two monstrous puppeteers take control of my limbs

(Stands up and walks away slowly) the only hope.

Pause.

PLAYWRIGHT: *(puts the glass on the bedside table)* I've been having the same nightmare most nights, since they banned my plays and threatened my producers, my crew, my friends, my family … I saw myself chained by each wrist, I'm pulled apart and my body is about to be torn into pieces. I struggle to get rid of the chains. The more movements I make, the more I'm pulled apart. I can see the blood gushing from the cracks of my chest and belly. I struggle to shout wildly and furiously… but they've muzzled me. *(After a short pause)* Eventually, the chains change into strings and two monstrous puppeteers take control of my limbs. They move my head, my hands, and my feet. They have control over all my actions and thoughts. They even speak for me. They move my lips and say the things I never meant. Then, their voice changes into whistles. They whistle so loudly that I can't take it anymore, I try to get rid of the strings, but the more movements I make, the more they take me under control.

(Shrill whistles are blown. Upstage left two men come into sight. Wearing white gloves, their heads and chests are not visible. A general wash of light illuminates the stage. DIRECTOR and COSTUME DESIGNER rush in. STAGE MANAGER receives a long sheet of paper, evidently a list, from the men and a black package, shakes hands with them and enters with a broad dazzling smile. He takes the sofa out of the stage, comes back with two chairs and puts one on the left and the other one on the right side of the stage. PLAYWRIGHT and ACTRESS approach the seats and sit down slowly. STAGE MANAGER first gives PLAYWRIGHT a Coca-Cola and ACTRESS a Fanta and an apple, and then takes out a large black veil from the package and spreads it over the ACTRESS and covers her entire body. Shrill piercing whistles are blown. Dead blackout.) ✖

PICTURED:
Dana Haqjoo and
Gehane Strehler
as Hamed Amiri's
parents in The
Boy with Two
Hearts at the
Wales Millennium
Centre

Why the Taliban wanted my brave mother dead …

Hamed Amiri's play The Boy with Two Hearts tells of his mother's campaign for women's rights and how the family fled Afghanistan. It is based on his memoir, an extract of which we publish overleaf. **MARK FRARY** reports

WHEN HAMED AMIRI was 10 years old he watched his mother Fariba give a speech in his hometown of Herat, Afghanistan, speaking out for women's rights and education and against the ruling Taliban.

A day later, a mullah gave the order for Fariba's execution and the family began a gruelling 18-month journey through Europe that ultimately saw them arrive in the UK in the back of a lorry. They were granted asylum and settled in Cardiff.

Over the next few pages, we publish an extract of Hamed's book, The Boy with Two Hearts, which tells of the family's escape from Afghanistan and their journey as refugees through Europe to the safety of Britain only to discover that Hamed's brother Hussein had a rare heart condition.

The story is uplifting but with a sad twist. The family reached safety but Hussein died from complications from his heart condition in 2018. Hussein's death inspired Hamed to write his memoir.

Now 32, Hamed works in IT and volunteers as a governor in the NHS that looked after his brother. He is regularly asked to tell the story of his family's journey as a motivational speaker.

ABOVE: Fariba's dramatic story unfolds on stage.

In October 2021, the Wales Millennium Centre produced and staged a theatre production of The Boy with Two Hearts which was adapted by Phil Porter and directed by Amit Sharma. Chris Wiegand, reviewing the play for The Guardian, said: "This is a show that deserves as wide an audience as possible, from schoolchildren to politicians." ✖

Mark Frary is associate editor at Index on Censorship →

50(04):60/65|DOI:10.1177/03064220211068703

 A day later, a mullah gave the order for Fariba's execution and the family began a gruelling journey through Europe

THERE WAS NOTHING special about our house in Herat, but it was all I knew as home until I was ten years old. It was built of clay, like all the other houses in our neighbourhood, and it was made up of four fairly bare rooms, with Persian rugs covering the floors. We lived with the families of two of my Dad's brothers, so it was always full and busy, and my brothers and cousins and I were always causing trouble.

There was a kitchen area where Mum would make kichiri, and a sitting and dining room with no sofas or dining chairs, only patterned pillows or nalincheh. We didn't eat our meals at a table, but around the sofra, an eating area on the floor.

The Taliban had taken control of Herat before I could remember, and rules in the city were strict. Curfew was 8pm. No one went out after dark, and women weren't allowed to go anywhere on their own. Even us children had to be careful who we spoke to, what we said and how we said it. The Taliban were everywhere, so it wasn't a good idea to do anything to stand out.

I was the middle of three boys, the jokey troublemaker sandwiched between my cheeky, liked-by-all older brother Hussein and my quieter, more reserved little brother Hessam, and we were sheltered from most of what went on with the Taliban. But I would sometimes overhear the elders talking about what they did – stories of mercenaries decapitating civilians and quickly sealing the neck with hot wax so they could bet on which headless body would stay standing the longest.

Then, one bright, and surprisingly warm winter's day when I was ten, everything changed. I had run home to fetch our football – a crumpled piece of lightweight PVC wrapped in another torn plastic bag – and as I went into the house I could hear Mum's voice from the kitchen. She was practising a speech she was writing. Word that this speech was happening had spread around the community, but in hushed voices.

'We have the same rights as men!' She paused, repeated herself quietly, and then shouted it. 'We have the same rights as men!'

This kind of talk was normal in our house, but I knew it spelt danger. Mum's interest in women's rights had begun a few years ago when some of the other mothers in the neighbourhood had asked her to mentor their teenage daughters.

Mum had a reputation for being an amazing cook, and she was brilliant at sewing. The neighbourhood mothers were keen for their daughters to learn the home skills they would need when they got married and, having only sons, Mum enjoyed teaching them. She treated them like daughters.

But as the girls she mentored came and went, Mum began to realise that once they got married they wouldn't be much more than servants for their new husbands. How could she prepare them for that? The Taliban rule meant that girls had few rights anyway – they weren't allowed to go to school and had no choice but to wear the full burka. Outside the home they were considered useless.

Mum was going to give her speech the next day, which was a Friday. The community would be coming together for Jummah, the Friday prayers, and as many people as possible would hear it. But that meant it wouldn't just be the women she was trying to help who would be listening; the Taliban would hear it too.

I watched from the living room as Mum moved around the kitchen, making the dinner and practising her speech. Then Dad came in.

Dad was Mum's biggest fan. He was always getting under her feet and bustling around the kitchen, but he always supported her. He didn't look like most Afghans – he was fairskinned with hazel eyes – and he had run a china shop with one of his brothers before opening the pharmacy where he now worked. Family was everything to him, and he backed Mum's ambitions to fight for female equality. But he also loved us all and wanted to protect his family, and he knew Mum's speech was dangerous. Opposing the Taliban publicly would put all of us in danger, and over the last few days we'd noticed his nerves starting to show.

'Where are the boys?' he said now. 'The whole neighbourhood knows about your speech. I really hope you know what you're doing.'

Mum looked up from the stove for a second and then turned back to what she was doing.

CREDIT: Wales Millennium Centre/Jorge Lizalde

PICTURED: The
Amiri family as
portrayed on
stage in Cardiff

'They're playing football,' she said. 'And don't worry about tomorrow – we have God on our side.'

I crept out and went to find my brothers.

* * *

That night we were all quiet around the sofra. Hessam and I sat either side of Hussein as usual, but instead of squabbling and joking we all quietly fidgeted on the rug. The food was delicious as always, but it was difficult to enjoy it as all I could think about was what might happen when Mum gave her speech tomorrow. Finally, Dad broke the silence.

'Can't you tone down the speech, Fariba? Be less critical of the Taliban?' Although Dad was proud of what Mum was doing, I could tell he was nervous about what might happen.

Mum was quick to defend her cause. 'Like they tone down their injustice? Have you forgotten how they threw boiling water at my own mother?' She looked at him defiantly, and we were all silent again.

'What about the children? At least think about them,' Dad said.

Mum was growing impatient. 'Think about the children? Okay. Do you want your children to grow up in an Afghanistan run by thugs? This isn't about us or our children, Mohammed. We need to take back what they have taken from us. We need to take back our future.'

Dad looked at us and then back to Mum. 'You know I'm with you to the end, don't you, Fariba?

Come what may? There's no going back now, that's all. God help us.'

As we carried on eating I looked across at Hussein. His lips were turning purple again. I quickly nudged Hessam, who made a gesture at Dad without Mum noticing. But when I looked back at Hussein I saw his colour returning.

Every night, Mum would tell us a story after tucking us in to bed. The three of us slept in the same small bedroom with its single barred window looking over the street. Mum would usually decide the story for us, but that night Hessam beat her to it.

'Mum, why did the Taliban throw hot water at grandmother? Does it give people fiery tempers like you?'

Mum settled herself at the foot of the bed, smiling. 'I'll tell you about your grandmother,' she said. 'There was a time in our city when there were schools just for girls, so they could get an education just like you. But the Taliban shut them down. Your grandmother – and others like her who fought for equal education – were violently humiliated...'

Grandma sounded like a fierce woman. I could see where Mum got it from. I wondered what I would fight for when I grew up.

The next day was Friday. As the three of us walked to school, neighbours, shopkeepers and acquaintances were quick to express their excitement for Mum's big day. We thanked each one nervously. 'We're so going to be taken hostage,' I said to Hussein, and he punched me.

Every street corner of our fifteen-minute →

→ walk felt like the end of the line. At school, the teacher wrote something on the blackboard about pomegranate seeds being like tiny rubies, but I couldn't concentrate. I was more focused on what the other boys were whispering. Even the class bullies were quieter today. Maybe they thought we were going to be taken hostage too.

Mum had told us to go straight to another school in the neighbourhood when the last bell rang. She would be giving her speech in the playground. As we walked through Herat there were women in the streets, lots of them, all heading the same way as us. There was a weird kind of energy, and I couldn't work out if this was good or bad. My imagination ran wild. Perhaps Taliban informers had betrayed Mum's cause and were plotting another massacre?

As we arrived at the school, we saw a makeshift podium that clearly was able to be dismantled as quickly as it was put up. The audience, almost all of them women, were still arriving and there was hardly any room left in the playground. I thought I was good at counting, but I started running out of hundreds as I scanned the crowd. Apparently we were guests of honour, and we were ushered to the front to watch as Mum got ready to climb the wooden step ladder to the podium. Suddenly she came over and crouched down beside us. Her hands were shaking.

'You know I love you all,' she said. Her voice was trembling too. I couldn't work out whether she was scared or excited, but she kissed us all on the forehead and told us again how much she loved us. What was this? Was she saying goodbye? Mum opened her speech with the usual 'God is great', and everyone went quiet. The people in the audience seemed as nervous as she was. I looked up at Mum and then at the crowd. People were nodding and shouting 'Inshallah!' ('God willing!') as she spoke about making family values part of our vision of a new Afghanistan. I'd heard other people talking about this, so it was nothing unusual. But for a woman to stand up and talk about it like this in public was unheard of – and dangerous.

The rest of the speech was a blur. I remember a few bits – the Taliban, unity, extremism, freedom

– and I remember the audience clapping and cheering. When Mum had nearly finished, she had to wait for the chants of 'Down with the Taliban' to stop before she could make herself heard. She finally ended by calling for unity and courage, and everyone clapped loudly.

Mum looked like a winner in a fight as she walked off the stage. We couldn't help but smile as she came towards us, and I felt so proud of her. Despite the laws on hugging and kissing in public, Dad gave her one of his signature bear hugs, and we giggled as the school headmaster ran over quickly to pull him away. Didn't Dad know that the rooftops of the houses all around had a view of the playground?

Mum kissed us again and I felt a sense of relief. But it didn't last long. Well-meaning supporters in the crowd were starting to surround Mum, jostling and pushing to get nearer. She tightened her grip on my hand. My other hand was holding Hussein's and I tightened my hold on him, trying not to fall over under all the people. I could hear voices asking Mum when they could visit her secretly. I could hardly stand up and the noise was terrifying.

'We must be cautious and smart …', I could hear her saying above the racket.

Then, as if by magic, the crowd disappeared. All those people were ready enough to rise to the challenge and make a difference, but they didn't want to be seen by the Taliban. It was fair enough. The Taliban were good at making examples of their enemies.

As we walked home Mum had never held our hands so tightly. We were proud of her, and I think she was proud of herself, but she seemed nervous. Everyone in the street was looking at us, nodding at Mum in support.

Mum's speech wasn't just about her of course, but we still felt proud of what she'd done. She'd been watching the cruelty of the Taliban for years, and now she'd finally been able to stand up to them.

Although it felt good to see how proud the neighbourhood was of Mum, we couldn't wait to get home. We walked through the narrow streets and alleyways, Dad hurrying us along like a shepherd. He kept fussing at how slowly we were walking, and rushed us impatiently. He only seemed to relax when we could see our front door.

He half pushed us into the house and, looking around, locked the door behind us. This was a first – our door was hardly ever locked. So many of us lived in our house that there were always aunties and uncles, cousins and neighbours making their way in and out. Even though Herat was ruled by the Taliban, ours was a relatively safe neighbourhood on a quiet road, and there didn't feel much need for locked doors.

But I could feel Dad's relief. He bustled around Mum, trying to distract her and keep us all busy. 'Let's have a celebration!' he said. 'Our favourite meal to mark the occasion. It's been a great day, a memory we'll never forget. A lesson of faith and belief.' This was all for our benefit of course – Dad wanting to show us it would all be okay. They didn't want to worry Hussein. But we weren't going to say no to our favourite dinner. While Mum prepared the meal, Dad kept his mind busy by watering the plants. He seemed on edge, but no matter how hard he tried, he couldn't hide the smile on his face.

We were a bit in awe of Mum that day. We'd never seen anyone stand up to the Taliban, let alone a woman. Mum's bravery was normal in our house, but this was the first time it had crossed into the outside world. We were proud. We couldn't stop talking about it, each going over our favourite part of the speech. For Hussein, it was seeing the faces of the women in the audience as they listened to Mum. For Hessam (mummy's boy), it was when Mum kissed him and made him feel like a VIP.

I said it was the moment at the end of the speech where, just for a second, I caught Mum's eye. I could see how happy she was, and I knew that she'd done something she really believed in. Mum wanted the little spark she'd created that day to grow into a big fire, and I wished she'd been able to do that.

We weren't expecting anyone, but when the knock at the door came we still thought it must be one of our uncles. Dad walked cautiously towards the door. We all hoped for a friendly face

as he asked loudly, 'Who is it?'

'It's me. Open the door, quick,' came a whisper. Relieved to hear the friendly voice of our uncle, or amu, Dad rushed to unlock the doors to embrace him. But we could tell something was up – his voice was panicked, and before Dad could even hug him or say hello he pushed the door shut behind him.

'Close the door, lock it!' he said. We'd never seen Uncle like this before. Dad looked worried.

'What is it? Is the family okay? Sister is unwell … how is her health?'

Uncle looked past Dad at us sitting at the sofra. We rushed up to hug him, but his smile was fake. Even without Dad's worried face in the background, we knew something was wrong. Uncle's hug was tighter and lasted longer than usual. Reluctantly we went into our bedroom to let the adults talk.

Hessam was being annoying, and Hussein tried to distract him while I tried to listen in to the adults' conversation. Uncle called Mum over, and we heard Dad say, 'Please, tell me what has happened. Is everyone okay?'

'They heard the speech,' he whispered. 'They're looking for you.'

'Okay,' said Dad. 'What else? Please, just tell us.'

Uncle spoke so quietly I could hardly make out what he said, but I heard, 'The mullah has given an order.'

This was it. All our fears in one sentence. We called the mullah the 'executioner', and we were terrified of him. He had turned our local football pitch into a place of execution, and it was now referred to as 'the pit'. People would gather there to hear death sentences passed on people who spoke up against the Taliban. Later they'd be executed. Someone must have told them about Mum, and now they wanted her dead. ✖

The Boy with Two Hearts is published by Icon Books (iconbooks.com, £16.99, ISBN 9781785786198)

Hamed Amiri was born in Herat, Afghanistan, and grew up under Taliban rule before escaping at the age of 10. He is a motivational speaker and a board member at Coleg Gwent

GAZIANTEP, CLOSE TO SYRIAN BORDER, TURKEY

URLA, TURKEY

The first steps: across Europe with Little Amal

JOE MURPHY and **JOE ROBERTSON** of Good Chance Theatre on their symbolic take on the long journey of refugees from Syria to the UK, which we follow in these pictures

WE RECENTLY ARRIVED home from an 8,000km walk, following a young girl. We knew her well — she was a character in our first play, The Jungle, which we wrote on our return from building and running the Good Chance Theatre in the Calais refugee camp of that name in 2015-16. This time, however, the girl was different. She had grown up. She was tall, very tall. On this journey, Little Amal was a giant puppet.

Her name means "hope" in Arabic, and we had hopes for her. We had hope that she had more to say than the one word ('school') that she spoke in The Jungle. We had hope that she could provide some sort of tonic or inspiration for those searching for refuge and those who welcome. And we also had hope that it might be easier to empathise, to connect with her – a young girl – than with the negative images of refugees so commonly shared in the media. →

PIRAEUS, GREECE

CHIOS, GREECE

VATICAN CITY

CREDIT: (Gaziantep) Hüseyin Ovayolu; (Urla) Andre Liohn; (Piraeus) Elina Giounanli; (Chios) Sokratis Baltagiannis; (Vatican City) handout

The moment that we knew something was working came when Amal, in a tired fit of rage in a village in Italy, yawned — and provoked a yawn from people in the crowd

NAPLES

STUTTGART

GENEVA

→ Designed by the incredible Handspring Puppet Company, and under the remarkable direction of Amir Nizar Zuabi, this summer she became real to many hundreds of thousands of people as she took a continent for her stage. Produced by Good Chance, Stephen Daldry, David Lan, Tracey Seaward and Naomi Webb, this epic play – too big for any single theatre – was called The Walk.

At 3.5 metres tall, she was impossible to ignore. But at that scale, she took on an appearance that felt more real than when we had first encountered her in our play. She wasn't the girl in need we had expected her to be. Rather, she was a leader, someone who we were destined to follow as she searched for her mother across Europe. Everywhere she passed through, she was welcomed by performances, feasts, events, offerings. The Walk was a provocation, a chance, a good chance, for every city, town and village along the main migration routes of Europe to demonstrate their perfect welcome – and to do it at scale.

She turned city centres into theatres, and the public became her audience, whether they were expecting it or not.

BELFORT, FRANCE

National Theatre

LONDON

DOVER

The moment that we knew something was working came when Amal, in a tired fit of rage in a village in Italy, yawned – and provoked a yawn from people in the crowd. This was the real connection we had dreamed of.

In theatres we are programmed to make these connections, to believe in the illusion. It is an expected ground for this kind of intense connection. But outside, in the real world, such intensity does not wash. It is not normal to cry at scenes in the streets of our towns. It is not normal to empathise with someone – however young – who is lost and looking for help. It is not normal to hold hands with audience members you have never met before. It is not normal to believe what could be the case.

Even before the pandemic, the feeling had arrived that we must be doing more to reach outside of our theatres. It is often the case in the world of art that we castigate ourselves for not doing enough "outreach". If we did more of it, we say, then more people would come into our theatres. But this is wishful thinking. The truth is, some people, lots of people, do not want to come into our theatres, and many have good reason. Theatres are clean, vast, opulently designed, expensive and intimidating. They are full of words, but often empty of both audience and meaning.

Perhaps there is another ingredient to add into our mix. The way in which Little Amal was welcomed by hundreds of artistic and civic groups is in an indication of what could be the case if theatre were not to root itself so firmly in its historic buildings. Forget just trying to persuade people to come and see shows. If theatre is to remain relevant in our social and political lives, perhaps it has to take its first steps outside its buildings, and back towards us? ✖

Joe Murphy and Joe Robertson are the co-founders of Good Chance Theatre

50(04):66/69|DOI:10.1177/03064220211068704

TURKEY FOCUS

Fighting Turkey's culture war

Theatres were shuttered in Istanbul following the Gezi Park protests in 2013 and repurposed as boutique hotels and campaign offices for the ruling AKP. But directors and playwrights have found ways around government attempts to stop the show, writes **KAYA GENÇ**

N 2012, AN ambitious theatre production debuted in Istanbul. Dubbed "the first-ever social media play," it concerned a president, and Pinima, the fictional country he ruled with an iron fist. Turning on their head fundamentals of democracy, the president allowed gender equality, but only between members of the same gender. Pinima's inflation was zero percent because the president reset it each morning. World leader in importing teargas to disperse dissenting crowds, Pinima allowed total freedom to citizens, on the condition that they realise it only in a private capacity. Tall and charismatic, Pinima's unnamed ruler

perpetually pontificated about his virtues to the masses and claimed to embody the "will of the nation." The only person bold enough to raise her voice against his demagoguery is a young pianist. When Pinima bans the use of the musical note E for its "feminine qualities" and destroys all its pianos to replace them with new ones that lack E notes, she decides to build a resistance movement.

Directed by Memet Ali Alabora, a Turkish actor famed for playing a cop in a popular 2000s TV show, Mi Minör featured 16 actors and was staged in two Istanbul venues (one was a basketball court) spacious enough to house its serpentine set. Alabora asked audiences

to film the play and tweet about it during the performance. Mi Minör's demand for participation led to colourful episodes. A woman threw her shoe to Alabora's head. Another teared up while witnessing police brutality. A few applauded the leader's autocratic speeches.

Just six months after Mi Minör's premiere, thousands filled Istanbul's Gezi Park to protest Turkey's authoritarian regime. On 10 June 2013, while crowds continued streaming protests on their smartphones, pro-government papers came up with an unprecedented theory. "Staged in Istanbul between 1 December 2012, and 14 April 2013, Mi Minör was a rehearsal of Gezi," one article

CREDIT: Jordi Boixareu/The Passenger/Alamy

PICTURED:
Protesters crowd
Taksim Square,
Istanbul, during the
Gezi Park uprising
in 2013.

Theatre companies came up with ingenious tactics to tackle Turkish autocracy

Thirteen different theatre venues in Istanbul's Beyoğlu quarter, once filled with eager audiences, have pulled the shutters down, 10 shortly after Gezi's suppression. "You could walk from Taksim Square to the tail end of Istiklal Avenue and spot a theatre in every corner," recalls Bahar Çuhadar, theatre critic for Turkey's leading daily Hürriyet.

Most of these venues were in former car repair shops and carwashes, laundries, dusty photography studios, former caravanserais, or inns. Nowadays, Olivia Han had been turned into a boutique hotel, and Rumeli Han, sold off. Taksim Stage, one of Istanbul's beloved theatre venues, famed for its medium-sized stage and central location, was repurposed as a party campaign office for the ruling AKP. It later became a Sofitel hotel. "People stopped frequenting Beyoğlu as it turned into a centre for shopping and tourism," says Çuhadar.

By the time Çuhadar started her career a decade ago, the view was different. She witnessed the birth of a new theatre climate in Turkey when her first review appeared in the leftist newspaper Radikal in July 2011.

"In 2010, independent and alternative theatres had blossomed. Not funded by Ankara or local municipalities, these small theatres supported themselves through ticket sales and began mushrooming in every corner." These groups resembled Europe's off-fringe theatre companies: "they were avant-garde, experimental, even revolutionary."

Spearheading the movement was DOT, a private company founded in 2005 by Murat Daltaban, Süha Bilal, and Özlem Daltaban. DOT quickly built a reputation with a flurry of in-yer-face plays, a genre that had already dated in Britain but was eagerly received in Turkey. Numerous English plays, freshly translated to Turkish, were staged in Istanbul's new black box stages.

Audiences who once abhorred theatre because of cumbersome, traditionalist plays now savoured the intimacy of small apartments where they watched passionate actors in their daily outfits arguing or kissing just a foot away. "There was a new language, a revolution in how actors interacted with audiences," says Çuhadar. "They talked about the most intimate, taboo subjects, like domestic violence or incest."

The founder of London's Arcola Theatre, Mehmet Ergen, was a key figure. His adaption of Lucy Kirkwood's It Felt Empty When the Heart Went at First But it is Alright Now, first staged in 2011, won critical acclaim. DOT's adaptation of David Ives's Venus in Fur turned into another box-office hit. Sarah Kane and Mark Ravenhill became household names among theatre lovers.

But soon, audiences became uneasy about this wave of imported plays. "We said: 'Enough with John and Mary's problems. Tell us something about our people!' It felt like constantly watching dubbed films," Çuhadar recalls. Local playwriting flourished in response. Sharing features of the in-yer-face style—tonally direct and attempting to grab audiences by the scruff of the neck to communicate their message—that emerged in the 1990s these plays pondered taboo topics: homosexuality, draft evasion, suppression of minorities, and others. Kurdish playwright and director Mirza Metin's Disko Number 5, for example, told torture sessions in Diyarbakır in the 1980s. This renaissance of a theatre of resistance was exciting but by no means unprecedented: plays by Melis Cevdet Anday or Adalet Agaoğlu also tackled similarly sensitive themes in recent past. "It was the tone of these →

claimed. "New information has emerged that casts doubt on the innocence of Gezi protesters, who are funded by the interest lobby in their attempt to turn protests into a global operation."

A concerted campaign to intimidate Mi Minör's crew forced Alabora to fear for his safety. Fleeing the country, he moved to Britain. After a court order for his immediate arrest in 2018, he's unlikely to return. Mi Minör's author Meltem Arıkan, charged with toppling the government, settled in Wales (you can read her story on page 73).

In the years following Mi Minör's debut, Turkey's theatre world remained defiant while licking its wounds.

→ new plays, what I call Turkish in-yer-face, that was different," says Çuhadar.

Still, these plays largely refrained from tackling Turkey's contemporary problems openly, instead excavating stories of inequality and violence from Turkey's past, when the secularist CHP, or military juntas ran Turkey.

But alarm bells rang when, in February 2012, the Turkish government came up with a "Turkey Art Council" project which planned to close down all state and municipality theatres. Claimed to be based on Arts Council England, it would fund each assignment separately. Fixed salaries and job security would vanish. Pro-government pundits were attempting to portray unwilling theatre workers as ungrateful elites misusing public funds. The theatre world's reaction was loud and powerful. A protest event, Freedom From Fear, collected hundreds in central Istanbul. One actor played the guitar while a director delivered a speech; the festive mood continued until the morning.

Mi Minor was born in this atmosphere. "It was the time of Wikileaks, Anonymous and Occupy," Meltem Arıkan, Mi Minör's playwright, told Index. "I witnessed how social media provided a platform to share our personal stories when traditional media remained silent." On social media, she noticed, "interactions happened regardless of the barriers of distance, language, nation, religion or ideology. This inspired me to create Mi Minor." As a playwright, she added, it was crucial to highlight how this affected the relationship between people and their government. "Men rule the analogue world, which is hierarchical.

Women, meanwhile, have always been governed through being forced into passivity. In the analogue era, our perception was shaped by whatever the media presented to us. But the transition to the digital suggests that whatever ideological, racial or religious differences there might be, individuals are liberating themselves from the logic of the herd and demanding the right to think freely and to express themselves freely." This idea of liberation from orthodoxies empowered Mi Minör and Gezi alike.

But the government's clampdown in late 2013 was unrelenting. Many actors had to flee Turkey in Gezi's wake. Fifteen theatres, including Genco Erkal's Dostlar Tiyatrosu, lost all their funding. Erkal could no longer stage his plays in Anatolia, as local administrators stopped him from performing. "Theatre people weren't afraid, but their support networks were," says Çuhadar. "And those who stayed didn't want to stage sterile plays or adopt British games any longer. They continued to act because they had something to say. All the plays we've seen since Gezi have been based on a foundation of dissent."

Over the next half-decade, the Turkish theatre's centre of gravity shifted from Beyoğlu to Kadıköy, where a slew of new companies came up with ingenious tactics to tackle Turkish autocracy. They took classic plays by Chekhov, Shakespeare, and others and adapted them in such a way that the texts conduct a secret dialogue about Turkey's contemporary ills. Bir Baba Hamlet, staged by Baba Sahne, is an important example. "It's a Hamlet adaptation, and on the surface, all the action takes place in Denmark," Çuhadar says. But the play ingeniously alluded to Turkey through Shakespeare's murderous villains. "The audience was experiencing a catharsis, and the hall echoed with slogans. I wouldn't be surprised if the police showed up at the door."

Between 2014 and 2021, Gezi-themed plays flourished. Mekan Sahne, an Ankara group, staged Nothing Will Be The Same Anymore, Clean Your Tears (2014), highlighting how the protests brought together young people who would otherwise never meet: a boy raised in an orphanage and a college graduate couple. In 2015, Ceren Ercan and Gülce Uğurlu's play The Unwanted pointed to interSpecial Reports of the Arab Spring and Gezi, interrogating how massive public events affect private lives. Another play, titled Karabatak, by Berkay Ateş, was devoted to people who died in Gezi. Ceren Ercan's I Love You Turkey was a trilogy, each instalment looking at lives forever changed by the uprising.

In 2018, a progressive politician, Ekrem İmamoğlu, won Istanbul's mayoral elections, and everything changed. The following year İmamoğlu appointed Arcola Theatre's Mehmet Ergen to the general art director position of the Istanbul Metropolitan Municipality City Theatre to the dismay of far-right supporters of the government who claimed, without evidence, that Ergen was a "terrorist supporter." During the pandemic, Ergen opened these stages to independent theatres to help them survive Covid's financial toil.

A decade after Mi Minör, Turkey's culture war continues. On 29 October 2021, AKM, the city's most celebrated stage, reopened. The honour of being the first writer to be staged there fell to Necip Fazıl Kısakürek, the Islamists' favourite playwright who was a far-right polemicist and the Turkish translator of The Protocols of the Elders of Zion. "There are lots of Sultan stories in state theatre's programme for this year," says Çuhadar. "I don't think AKM's directors even know the names of Turkey's new generation of independent playwrights." Still, she remains hopeful. "The young theatre makers we supported a decade ago are now in their 40s. The seeds we planted a decade ago are sprouting." ✖

Kaya Genç is contributing editor (Turkey) for Index. He is based in Istanbul.

Many actors had to flee Turkey in Gezi's wake. Fifteen theatres lost their funding

50(04):70/72|DOI:10.1177/03064220211068705

I wrote a play then lost my home, my husband and my trust

Turkish playwright **MELTEM ARIKAN**'s Mi Minör was blamed for the seminal Gezi Park protests that convulsed Istanbul

ABOVE: Arıkan's play generated huge publicity but critics said she was part of a secret international conspiracy against Turkey

AM A WOMAN kicked out of Heaven.

I am a writer tried for treason, facing life in prison.

I am an exile defined as others.

I am autistic, pushing myself to be normal.

Only to become invisible.

I'm 52 years old. Since childhood, I have always felt alienated from my environment. The more petulant I became, the more walls I built between myself and the world, the greater the desire to flee grew. Not knowing from whom and from what I'm running away, only having the desire to shelter somewhere else, anywhere else. It is hard to be weird and different to others but not know why.

It has done irreparable damage to my self-esteem. I felt trapped inside a cocoon woven of my unhappiness. I was a thing apart. Other people were strictly separate from me. I felt this separation keenly.

This distinction was so clear in my childhood, as a young girl and even now it is the same…

For years, I established completeness in my inner world with all my broken fragments. Without expectation, motionless, distant, introverted. I drowned in words, definitions, tasks… I forgot my essence. I learned to mask myself because I have always been judged.

I have a lot of voices in my mind, ghosts of decades-old voices. Telling me how I should be…

In 2011 I wrote an absurd play called Mi Minör set in a fictional country called Pinima. During the performance, the audience could choose to play the President's deMOCKracy game or support the Pianist's rebellion against the system. The Pianist starts reporting all the things that are happening in Pinima through Twitter, which starts a role-playing game (RPG) with the audience. Mi Minör was staged as a play where an actual social media-oriented RPG was integrated with the physical performance. It was the first play of its kind in the world.

A month after our play finished, the Gezi Park demonstrations in Istanbul started. On 10 June 2013, the pro-government newspaper Yeni Şafak came out bearing the headline 'What A Coincidence', accusing Mi Minör of being the rehearsal for the protests, six months in advance. The article continued, "New information has come to light to show that the Gezi Park protests were an attempted civil coup" and claimed that "the protests were rehearsed months before in the play called Mi Minör staged in Istanbul".

After Yeni Şafak's article came out,

the mayor of Ankara started to make programmes on TV specifically about Mi Minör, mentioning my name.

In one he showed an edited version of one of the speeches that I made six years ago about secularism, misrepresenting what I said in such a way that it looked like I was implying that secularism was somehow antagonistic to religion.

What I found so brutal was that the mayor did this in the knowledge that religion has always been one of the most sensitive subjects in Turkey. What upset me most was the fear I witnessed in my son's eyes and the anxiety that my partner was living through.

The play was being discussed regularly on TV, websites and online forums and both Mi Minör and my →

For three nightmarish months, we were trapped in our own house and did not set foot outside

CREDIT: Payidar Şeyma

RIGHT: "I feel this land always wrapped itself around me," says Meltem Arıkan, pictured near her home in the Elan Valley in mid Wales

→ name were being linked to a secret international conspiracy against Turkey and its ruling party, the AKP. Many of the comments referenced the 2004 banning of my book Stop Hurting my Flesh. I received hundreds of emails and tweets threatening rape and death as a result of this campaign.

For three nightmarish months, we were trapped in our own house and did not set foot outside. One day, I saw that one of my prominent accusers was tweeting about me for four hours. The sentences he chose to tweet were all excerpts from my research publication The Body Knows, taken out of context and manipulating what I had written. Those tweets were the last straw.

I left our house, our loved ones, our pasts. We left in a night with a single suitcase and came to Wales, which had always been my dream country. I never imagined my arrival in Cardiff would be like this; feeling bitter, broken and incomplete.

Two years later my partner, who had remained in Turkey, and I got married. In the first month, I learned my husband had brain cancer. Operations, chemotherapy, radiotherapy followed... Within a year, I lost him. I visited him, but sadly I wasn't able to go to his funeral because of new accusations levelled against me. This was a turning point in my life. I lost my husband. I lost my trust in people. I lost my savings to pay for his care. I lost everything.

In all of this emotional turmoil, I started walking every day for five or six hours. Geese became my best friend and my remedy. I walked for months. I walked and walked everywhere, in the mountains, in the valleys, at the seaside.

These walks had a transformative effect on me. I had discovered a way to live as a woman who had learned to accept herself, rather than a shattered

and a lost woman.

Maybe there is an umbilical cord, beyond my consciousness, between me and the wild nature of Wales. I feel this land always wrapped itself around me, talked to me like a mother during the difficult time in my life. For this reason, I wrote my latest play; Y Brain/ Kargalar (Crows), written in Welsh and Turkish and produced by Be Aware Productions. It describes my story, the special place this land has in my life and how it transformed me. The title refers to my constant companions during this

time – the crows. One reviewer called it "unashamedly lyrical...even as it touches on dark themes".

On 20 February 2019, as the play was being staged, a new indictment was issued against 16 people, including me, over Mi Minör; I now face a life sentence. Because of this absurd accusation, I feel ever more strongly that Wales is protecting me.

It was at this time that I was diagnosed with Asperger's syndrome/ autistic spectrum disorder and I've received many answers about myself

I have therapy twice a week and I have started to understand what I have been through all my life. My therapists told me that I was manipulated and I was emotionally and sexually abused by whom I love and trust the most; it was a big shock for me. I spent half of my life trying to help abused victims, and I never thought I was a victim. They said this is very common because autistic women are not aware of when they were used. How could I have been so blind?

I couldn't work out that I was being played by others, like a fish on a line. As an autistic, communication is about interpreting with a basic belief in what people tell me because I don't tell lies myself. But I have learned how much capacity for lies exists. Autistic people can be gullible, manipulated and taken advantage of. But I learned that regret is the poison of life, the prison of the soul.

The most significant benefit of this process is that I am learning again like a child to re-evaluate everything with curiosity and enthusiasm. It also gives me the chance to reconstruct the rest of my life without hiding myself, being subjugated to anyone, and living without fear.

Autism diagnosis and discovery were liberating for me. There is still not enough autism spectrum awareness even today. That is why I decided to come out about my autism. I strongly believe that if those of us who are on the autistic spectrum share our experiences openly, then it wouldn't only help other autistic people, it would help neurotypical people to better understand both us and our behaviour.

Looking back at the last few years, I have been thrown into navigating most of the challenging aspects and life experiences and there has been a complete cracking of all masks.

This process is not easy at all, sometimes my soul, sometimes my heart, sometimes all my cells hurt, but it also causes me to recognise a liberation I have never known before.

Fortunately, during this process, I have been learning a lot about myself

I received hundreds of emails and tweets threatening rape and death

and how I have masked myself as an Aspie-woman... For me, masking myself is more harmful even than not knowing I'm autistic. Masking means that I create a different Meltem to handle every situation. I have never felt a strong connection with my core. When I am confronted with emotional upset, my brain immediately goes into "fix it" mode, searching for a way to make the other person feel better so I can also relieve my own distress.

For most of my life, I've allowed myself to fit in with how I thought others wanted me to feel and act, especially those I loved. My dark night gave me so much pain I broke free and started to care for myself and heal. Taking me back to my primordial self, not the heroic one that burns out, to step back from the battle line of existence, to remember the gods and spiritual parts of nature, my own nature and the person I was at the beginning.

The last two years have been exciting for me. It is as if I died and was reincarnated again. In the end, I understand that my true nature is not to be some ideal that I have to live up to. It's ok to be who I am right now, and that's what I can make friends with and celebrate. I learned it's about finding my own true nature and speaking and acting from that. Whatever our quality is, that's our wealth and our beauty. That's what other people respond to. I'm not perfect, but I'm real... ✖

Meltem Arıkan is a novelist and playwright

50(04):73/75|DOI:10.1177/03064220211068706

as a result. From this moment, a new discovery and understanding started. I set out to discover myself with this new knowledge. As soon as I could know who I'm not, I could find out who I am.

I realise that my wiring system simply makes it harder for me to do many things that come naturally to other people. On the flip side, it is important to be aware that autism can also give me many magical perceptions that many neurotypicals simply are not capable of. I believe I was able to write Mi Minör because of my different perceptions.

ABOVE: Banned playwright and novelist Ngugi wa Thiong'o, pictured with his son Thiongo in London in 2013, was pivotal in the fight against colonialism

Where silence is the greatest fear

ISSA SIKITI DA SILVA looks at how Kenyan theatre has suffered under a succession of corrupt rulers, hot on the heels of colonial repression

THE CULTURE OF protest and resistance in Kenya through the arts has come a long way. It can be traced back to the brutal and violent colonial rule of the British but, because of a lack of money, fundamental liberties and freedom of expression, most Kenyan artists kept largely silent.

The theatre in those days was run by white settlers who developed plays according to their values.

There was hope that Jomo Kenyatta's ascension to the presidency in 1964 would help heal the wounds inflicted by the British and pave the way to tolerance,

social justice, freedom and prosperity. But his presidency, characterised by an increasing centralisation of executive power and the repression of political opponents, prompted many artists to use the theatre as a tool to hammer what they saw as a neo-colonial government.

Playwright and novelist Ngugi wa Thiong'o led the pack with his first short plays – The Black Hermit (1962) and This Time Tomorrow (1968) – which sent a message to the people that nothing good was going to come out of the Kenyatta presidency. If The Trial of Dedan Kimathi (1976), co-written

with Micere Githae Mugo, painted the picture of Kenya's future artistic protest, Ngaahika Ndeenda (I Will Marry When I Want), co-written with Ngugi wa Mirii in 1977, set Kenyatta's presidency on fire.

The provocative play, written in his native Kikuyu language, angered the Kenyatta regime, which banned it and ordered Ngugi's detention. Undeterred by his one-year imprisonment, which appears to be what radicalised him, Ngugi continued his protest right through the Daniel arap Moi regime (1978-2002), often considered the country's most brutal, undemocratic and corrupt.

His critical play about colonial oppression, Maitu Njugira (Mother Sing to Me), in 1982 – again co-written with wa Mirii, and in collaboration with the Kamiriithu theatre community – was battered and banned by an intransigent

Moi, who subsequently ordered the open-air theatre where the drama was due to be played to be razed. Ngugi fled the country.

Moi, who ruled the east African nation with an iron-fist for 24 years, stood in the way of any kind of artistic protest by, among other ways, using arbitrary detentions to stifle activist theatre creativity. A theatre group called 5Cs (five years of colonialism) bore the brunt of Moi's corrupt and repressive regime.

Fredrick Odhiambo Ayieko, 5Cs secretary, told Index that the group developed plays that advocated good governance and leadership, democracy, gender equality, respect of human rights and nationhood and constitutional change. "We staged them in open spaces like shopping centres, markets, churches and bus stations, among others," he said.

Feeling that the plays were too critical of his presidency and therefore constituted a threat to his regime, Moi went on the offensive. Ayieko said: "Since we were operating under an oppressive regime, our plays exposed the government's wrongdoings and made a significant impact on society."

Angry and agitated by this form of artistic militancy, the government ordered the arrest of 5Cs members, who were subsequently jailed. Charges included illegal gathering and releasing toxic content to the public.

A wave of arrests which started in 1997 went on until 2007, through the presidency of Mwai Kibaki – who replaced Moi in 2002, promising mountains of freedom and zero corruption.

Denying or drying up funding to critical artists serves to ensure they do not thrive

The critical plays that led to six 5Cs members being arrested in 2000 were Dying to Be Free (about human rights violations) and Paukwa (depicting land issues). Other critical plays included Uhuru na Mashamba (Freedom and Land), Hawkers, Ufisadi (Corruption) and Democracy.

Corruption, one of the scourges that Kenyan artists were decrying through their creative work, is one of the country's biggest obstacles to development. The country ranked 124 out of 180 in the Transparency International 2020 report.

Expectations were high that freedom of expression would improve and corruption would be eradicated under Uhuru Kenyatta, who replaced Mwai Kibaki (another corrupt leader) in 2013. Civil society organisations had lambasted Kibaki for lacking commitment to fight and being complicit with corrupt individuals. But Kenyatta seemed determined to show anyone criticising his regime that some of Moi's blood still circulated in his veins.

Muthuri Kathure, Article 19's eastern Africa senior programme officer for civic space, confirmed that Kenya was still in the same position. He told Index: "One of the cases that we are involved in is [that] of [Edwin] Mutemi Kiama, who was arrested in 2020 for publishing information about how the presidential family benefited from public resources."

Kathure said artists in other fields had also been threatened with arrest, including Eric Omondi, for his show Wife Material. Kikuyu singer Muigai wa Njoroge was also arrested on allegations of hate speech for a political song criticising the president.

The arts were a powerful tool of informing masses, he said. By arresting and muzzling artists, governments risked calls for accountability.

Shepherd Mpofu, professor of media, culture and communications at the University of Limpopo in South Africa, concurred. He told Index that arts and

the theatre played a critical role that should not be undermined. But he said: "Governments have managed to oppress and almost drive artists off the stage. We should be alive to the fact that economic meltdown in most countries has affected the arts and therefore silenced a critical protest voice in society."

As well as facing a crackdown from the government and influential people and the harassment of artists through trumped up charges and physical abuse, theatre in Kenya faces funding challenges. Because of a lack of money, many groups, including 5Cs, are forced to scale down their activities and, unless they urgently get funding, they risk disappearing in the near future.

"It cannot be that directors, writers and actors have failed. A multiplicity of problems militates against them and this leads to their silencing," said Mpofo, who added that art had always been purposeful in Africa and rarely simply art for art's sake.

Here, silencing artists can take many forms, including "silencing in silence", as one Kenyan artist, who spoke on condition of anonymity, put it.

"Denying or drying up funding to critical artists serves to ensure that they do not thrive. What can you do when the government uses public resources to fund artists that sing its praises and overlook those that criticise it? You become frustrated and get stuck and simply disappear from the stage."

Ayieko added: "The government receives funding from the donor community for advocacy work but only channels it to government user-friendly groups. Any group that is criticising the government cannot access the money.

"Funding, or not funding, might be one way of censoring and silencing theatre. As theatre people, we are still cautious." ✖

Issa Sikiti da Silva is an Index on Censorship contributing editor based in west Africa

50(04):76/77|DOI:10.1177/03064220211068707

Censorship is still in the script

JONATHAN MAITLAND says that British theatre has lost its backbone and needs to be more courageous

N JUNE 2015, a national newspaper in Britain started a campaign to have a play banned. This surprised me for two reasons. One: clearly no one had told the Daily Mirror about the Theatre Act 1968, which abolished the state's censorship of the stage and did away with the quaintly repressive (if that's not an oxymoron) notion of the Lord Chamberlain's red pen. Two: the play in question was mine.

I wrote An Audience With Jimmy Savile to show how the late entertainer managed to get away with a lifetime of sexual offending. But despite the play's very public service intentions, the Mirror started a petition to stop it. And so, for a moment, I found myself in some exalted, unwarranted company: Ibsen and George Bernard Shaw had plays banned (Ghosts and Mrs Warren's Profession, respectively). Inevitably, however, the Mirror's cack-handed attempt at censorship failed and the play went ahead.

The episode was instructive, however. Because while it's true that "we" – that is, the British state – don't ban plays any more, a powerful and unhealthy censorious reflex still exists and there are clear signs that the urge to stifle and to repress has been growing stronger over the last few years. That repression takes many forms: a social media backlash here, a not-very-subtle government threat there – but it's real, it's unhealthy and it's profoundly worrying.

We are not, of course, in the same league as China – where a play bemoaning their treatment of Uyghur Muslims, for example, would never be

LEFT: The flashy symbols of disgraced showman Jimmy Savile, subject of Jonathan Maitland's play

officially sanctioned – but as playwright David Hare told me in an email exchange for this article, censorship in the West is real. It just isn't called that anymore.

"Is there censorship in the sense that there is censorship in Iran, Russia or China? Of course not. Nobody's physical survival is threatened," he said.

But he does seem to say that the BBC has, in effect, become a censorious government's useful idiot. (My phrase, not his.)

"The BBC has a current policy of deliberately not alienating the government," he said. "They have chosen the path of ingratiation rather than asserting their independence. The result is, effectively, a range of subjects [which is] hopelessly narrowed. Hence the ubiquity of cop shows. Even medical dramas are forbidden if they stray into questions of ministerial health policy."

Some might accuse Hare of pique, given that a TV adaptation of his most recent play, Beat the Devil, starring Ralph Fiennes, was turned down by the BBC. He says it was rejected because of the subject matter: Covid-19. (Hare became gravely ill with the virus and the play depicts him on his sickbed, despairing of the government's response to the pandemic as they "stutter and stumble" on the airwaves.)

Indeed, when Hare went public with his attack on the corporation for turning him down, it refused to comment and the inference was that this was an editorial judgment and not a political one. But, says Hare, they would say that wouldn't they?

"Censorship in the West," he said, occurs "in the impossible grey area between editorial judgment and active prohibition."

He's right. The most egregious recent example of censorship-in-all-but-name occurred in 2015 when the National Youth Theatre (NYT) cancelled a production of the play Homegrown, about the radicalisation of young Muslims, two weeks before it was due to open. The executive who made the

ABOVE: Putting Nadine Dorries in charge of culture in Britain is "a bit like getting Herod to run the local nursery"

decision cited "editorial judgment" as a factor.

But, thanks to Freedom of Information requests from Index on Censorship, a fuller explanation emerged soon afterwards. An email from the NYT executive responsible for cancelling the production contained the following line: "At the end of the day we are simply 'pulling a show' … at a point that still saves us a lot of emotional, financial and critical fallout."

In other words: "Yes, we might be censoring an important piece of work featuring the two most underrepresented groups on stage – Muslims and young people – because we are worried about defending ourselves from a backlash which hasn't happened yet, but we don't really fancy defending free speech and trying to ride out the storm because it's too much hassle. So, let's just cancel it and put it down to editorial judgment. Oh yeah – and safeguarding. Even

though putting on work like this should be our raison d'etre."

The director of the piece, Nadia Latif, was understandably shellshocked. A few weeks after the cancellation she said the creative team were "genuinely still reeling. The gesture of someone silencing you is a really profound one. You give your heart and soul to something, and someone comes and shuts it down. It's like they're saying my thoughts and feelings are no longer valid."

And to refer the audience to my earlier point, it's happening more and more. Albeit behind the scenes, and sometimes in ways you don't get to hear about. There are two reasons for this: the pandemic and the nature of the current government.

The pandemic first. Although Hare's Covid-19 polemic made it to the stage, that was the exception not the rule. I can't find any other examples of plays critical of the current government being either staged or commissioned.

That would seem to be directly related to the fact that, during lockdown, every theatre in the country was desperate →

You give your heart and soul to something and someone comes and shuts it down

➔ for financial assistance from the Treasury. So regrettably, but perhaps not surprisingly, few gave the go-ahead to works which bit, or even nibbled, the only hand that could feed them.

This isn't speculation. When the producers of my play The Last Temptation of Boris Johnson – an unashamed takedown of the prime minister – tried to book it into theatres for a national tour post-pandemic, more than one theatre said, in effect: "We are worried we will lose our Covid grants if we put on a play like that."

Which brings us on to the current Conservative government and its attempt to take a long march through our cultural, creative and editorial institutions.

When the Tories couldn't get the former Daily Mail editor Paul Dacre installed as the new boss of the broadcasting regulator Ofcom, they simply scrapped the selection process and ordered that it start again, putting Dacre's name forward once more – even though, first time round, the selection panel described him as "not appointable". Dacre has now voluntarily withdrawn and gone back to the Mail.

Someone who was appointable and acceptable, however – to the

government, that is – was Nadine Dorries, the new secretary of state for digital, culture, media and sport. Putting Dorries in charge at DCMS was a bit like getting Herod to run the local nursery. Within days of taking over she reportedly started issuing threats against our premier creative organisation – the BBC – which, in her view, was guilty of not sufficiently toeing the line.

After the BBC radio presenter Nick Robinson hectored Johnson in an interview – "Stop talking, prime minister" – it's said that Dorries told her advisers that Robinson had "cost the BBC a lot of money".

A bit like the take on Aids policy from the satricial show Brass Eye – is it Good Aids or Bad Aids? – there is Good Censorship and Bad Censorship. The decision to ban Homegrown falls into the latter category.

But the act of self-editing – in effect, self-censorship – has more going for it. As Hare puts it: "There is all sorts of subject matter I wouldn't tackle – but entirely because I'm not good enough. I have always refused anything which represents life in Nazi concentration camps, since I don't trust myself to do it well enough to do justice to what happened. If I don't

think I can do justice to the real suffering of real people, then I avoid, [although] I take my hat off to great writers who are able to expand subject matter at a level where it vindicates the idea of writing about absolutely everything. More power to them."

But it's complicated, of course. The worry is that more and more writers, terrified of a vicious social media backlash, are self-editing to an extent that is unhealthy. There are few, for example, who would now dare to pen a play that took a critical, coolly objective look at both sides of the argument over transgender rights – even though tackling difficult subjects and representing "problematic" points of view is, arguably, one of theatre's prime functions. What could be more relevant, and on point, than a play like that?

One playwright who did sail into these waters was Jo Clifford. Her play, The Gospel According to Jesus, Queen of Heaven, casts Jesus as a trans woman. During its 2018 run at Edinburgh's Traverse Theatre, an online petition demanding the play be banned garnered a healthy – or rather unhealthy – 24,674 signatures. Soon after that she spoke of how artists and writers were "on the front line of a culture war that will only deepen and strengthen as the ecological and financial crisis worsens and the right feel more fearfully that they are losing their grip on power".

So, at a time when writers and playwrights need to be bolder, the signs are that they're becoming more and more cowed; hence Sebastian Faulks's bizarre announcement that he will no longer physically describe female characters in his novels. Fortunately, most of his peers seem to disagree with him. A recent open letter signed by more than 150 eminent writers, artists and thinkers including JK Rowling, Margaret Atwood and Gloria

LEFT: Jo Clifford's play The Gospel According to Jesus, Queen of Heaven, which cast Jesus as a trans woman, ran into a storm of protest

RIGHT: Howard Brenton's 1980 play The Romans in Britain, which featured a homosexual rape, was unsuccessfully prosecuted for gross indecency

Steinem warned of "a fear spreading through arts and media".

"We are already paying the price in greater risk aversion among writers, artists and journalists who fear for their livelihoods if they depart from the consensus, or even lack sufficient zeal in agreement," it said.

Then again, not everyone agreed with the letter. Author Kaitlyn Greenidge said she was asked to sign it but refused, saying: "I do not subscribe to [its] concerns and do not believe this threat is real. Or at least I do not believe that being asked to consider the history of anti-blackness and white terrorism when writing a piece, after centuries of suppression of any other view in academia, is the equivalent of loss of institutional authority."

Like I said, it's complicated.

The big question for writers, then, is this – if, like me, you believe that anything goes on stage, provided it's not proscribed by law, how far should you go? Where do the (self-imposed) limits of free expression lie? Those limits are different for each writer, of course. I would draw the line at, for example, depicting sexual assault on stage. My Jimmy Savile play showed the effects of it, clearly, on the main character – a young woman who'd been abused by him at Stoke Mandeville Hospital – but left the rest to the audience's imagination. Sometimes it's more powerful that way.

I would, however, defend the right of other playwrights to go further and include vivid scenes of sexual assault, provided it was for the "right" reasons. There would need to be a coherent

dramatic justification for it and the creative team would be advised to have plenty of flak jackets ready. Anyone who tests the boundaries in this way will inevitably face accusations of prurience, unjustified provocation or worse.

In 1980, when Howard Brenton showed a scene of homosexual rape in The Romans in Britain, the production found itself being prosecuted for gross indecency by Mary Whitehouse as part of her attempt to "clean up" Britain. (The prosecution failed when a key witness admitted that, from the back of stalls, what he thought was a penis might have been an actor's thumb.)

A similar court case today would be unlikely. But then again there is always the Court of Public Opinion, powered by the rotten fuel of social media, which is arguably more scary and intimidating than the real thing.

I wouldn't draw the line at giving free expression on stage to anti-Semitism,

either. Sometimes the best way to destroy an argument is to bring it into the light. With one crucial proviso, which I will come to in a moment.

As a Jew who lost relatives in the Holocaust I am fascinated by the subject. I would love to see a play which explained where anti-Semitism came from. Or whether the definitions of it are justified. Are there internal contradictions there? (We fought the war to preserve our freedoms, but isn't using the label "anti-Semitic" a destruction of one of our most cherished freedoms? As in, the freedom of speech?)

Any play which seeks to answer these questions would need characters espousing anti-Semitism – the more articulately the better, in my view – if they are to work properly.

My proviso would be that the anti-Semitism would need to be both contextualised and rigorously challenged. This could be done within the play – two characters arguing – or in the form of a post-show debate.

I would, for example, even have defended the right of writer Jim Allen and director Ken Loach to stage Perdition, their controversial 1987 →

We are worried we will lose our Covid grants if we put on a play like that

→ play for the Royal Court, despite its disgusting anti-Semitic tropes.

The play accused Jews of "collaborating" with the Nazis during the Holocaust (is there a more loaded, insulting, inappropriate word in this context than "collaborated"?) and was based on the story of Rudolf Kastner, who negotiated with Adolf Eichmann to let more than 1,600 Jews flee Hungary for the safety of Switzerland.

Kastner, it is argued, should have done more to warn more Jews (not just the 1,600 that he rescued) of what was happening. Hence Allen's line: "To save your hides, you [a Jew] practically led them to the gas chambers." Disgusting, misjudged and morally wrong.

In the resulting furore, the Royal Court cancelled the play. But the decision to ban it, paradoxically, only increased support for it, and the poison

BELOW: David Hare's play Beat the Devil, about his battle with Covid-19, was rejected by the BBC but then staged in London, starring Ralph Fiennes

Repression takes many forms: a social media backlash here, a not-very-subtle government threat there

it contained. I would have let it go ahead but tried to persuade Allen to make editorial changes. And if that didn't work (and I doubt it would have done, although some controversial lines were excised during rehearsals) then I would have staged a debate, forming part of the show, which allowed the Jewish community to explain why the play was so offensive and misjudged. Education beats defenestration, every time.

The stage would be the perfect place to explore the arguments on both sides, but in particular to highlight the muddy thinking of the anti-Israel lobby, as personified by Sally Rooney, who recently decided to punish the Jews by forbidding a Hebrew translation of her latest novel. (Although making them read it might

have been a more effective punishment.)

British theatre is not in a good place today. Where are the revolutionaries? The new, angry young men and women, the new John Osbornes? We don't need to Look Back In Anger: it's all in front of us, now.

Would a film like 2009's Four Lions, a deeply moral but, to some, hugely offensive Jihadi satire, get made today? I very much doubt it.

We – all of us: writers, commissioners and directors – need to be braver. ✖

Jonathan Maitland is a journalist and play-wright. He is now working on a play about the British guitarist Wilko Johnson

50(04):78/82|DOI:10.1177/03064220211068709

82 INDEXONCENSORSHIP.ORG

CREDIT: Manuel Harlan

ABOVE: Ivam Cabral, from Os Satyros, performing in the play Aurora, which opened in the city of São Paulo in November 2021.

God waits in the wings … ominously

A presidential decree that art must be 'sacred' has cast a free-speech shadow over Brazilian theatre. **GUILHERME OSINSKI** and **MARK SEACOMBE** report

JAIR BOLSONARO, THE populist right-wing president of Brazil, has put the fear of God into playwrights and theatre companies across the nation.

While the overt and ruthless censorship of the military dictatorship that ended in 1985 is now history, theatre today has to comply with a nebulous concept known as "sacred art" or be starved of public funds.

Bolsonaro came to power in 2019 on a promise of "Brazil above everything, God above all" and was soon issuing a veiled warning to the theatre world that "certain kinds of works" would not be tolerated.

"We won't chase anyone, but Brazil has changed," he said. "With public funds we won't see certain kinds of works here. This isn't censorship, this is preserving Christian values, treating our youth with respect, recognising the traditional family."

In order to qualify for the public money on which theatre depends, plays and playwrights would now need to adhere to "sacred art". And representatives of this "sacred art" would make decisions about funding under the federal Rouanet law, introduced in 1991 to provide funds for art and culture, including film. In a country that is nominally 81% Christian, "sacred" could mean only one thing.

Although Bolsonaro's government is not imposing direct censorship, it is systematically dismantling theatre in Brazil by cutting off funding, according to Jader Alves, a theatre director at Lala Schneider, in Curitiba, capital of the southern state of Paraná.

"The federal government is pushing theatre into a corner," he says. "Not enabling incentive mechanisms to obtain financial resources is still censorship. If you're not supporting that area, maybe you don't want it to go forward."

And all this is during the Covid-19 pandemic, which, he says, has "killed" Brazilian theatre.

His views are shared by Ivam Cabral and Rodolfo García Vázquéz, founders in 1989 of the renowned theatre

Ignorance has reached a point that is unacceptable. We are scared

company Os Satyros in São Paulo, the biggest city in Brazil.

Asked if there is censorship affecting national theatre, Cabral says, without hesitation: "The answer is 'Yes' – in big capital letters."

One victim of censorship was Caranguejo Overdrive, an overtly political play, produced by Aquela Companhia de Teatro, which was critical of Brazilian presidents including Bolsonaro. A performance scheduled to celebrate the 30th anniversary of the state-run Bank of Brazil in 2020 was cancelled after the federal government in Brasilia intervened, but it was staged elsewhere later, including in Rio de Janeiro.

Plays which question the government or its right-wing values are not even considered for funding under the Rouanet law.

"This is a witch-hunt way of doing things. It's too sad," says Cabral. "We started to see religious theatre, religious music."

For Vázquéz, the viciously homophobic Bolsonaro is systematically attacking and censoring minorities, including the LGBTQ community.

And Alves says that, in the eyes of the president, homosexuality is associated with pornography and promiscuity and not seen as a suitable subject for theatre audiences with Christian values.

After the introduction of God and "sacred art" into the Rouanet law, there has been another regressive change whose meaning is less than clear. One of the law's purposes had been to help to eradicate prejudice and discrimination in all its forms. But in July 2021, this was altered and now it seeks to promote cultural citizenship, artistic accessibility and diversity.

"This is vague," says Alves. "We have diversity, but what does it mean? Are you talking about cultural diversity,

sexual diversity? Previously we had explicit terminology. For me this is censorship – very veiled, of course."

Vázquéz says public notices from the federal government make clear that it favours, and prioritises, religious plays – especially those praising the traditional family.

"Ignorance has reached a point that is unacceptable. We are scared. It looks as if we are living in the 19th century."

How did Brazil get to this point? To understand how South America's most populous country – 212.5 million people at the last count – arrived here, it helps to look back at the history of Brazil, where culture has never been one of the government's big concerns, says Alves.

Censorship of theatre today was linked to the country's past and to colonial rule under the Portuguese. ➔

ABOVE: With God on his side – allegedly – President Jair Bolsonaro has been accused of veiled censorship of theatre. He has also been widely criticised for his verbal attacks on women, the black population and LGBTQ people

→ "When John VI of Portugal [King of Brazil from 1816 to 1822] arrived here, he built opera houses, which didn't exist in Brazil, and then he had theatre companies brought from Lisbon to perform for him," he says. "Instead of fostering the development of local companies, he found it easier to bring it from Portugal."

For this reason, local art was not encouraged; nor were the conditions created for it to flourish, and to be appreciated, across the country.

Cabral concurs. "We have no memory. What Brazil has already produced from geniuses is impressive," he says. "Even Satyros is much more respected outside Brazil. Here it seems that we are just another one out there."

In the dark days of the military

dictatorship between 1964 and 1985 – when an estimated 20,000 people were tortured and hundreds killed – the arts were heavily censored through the Department of Federal Censorship.

After the fall of the regime, the arts were liberated and, in 1985, Brazil set up an autonomous Ministry of Culture for the first time. But one of Bolsonaro's first acts in 2019 was to abolish it.

"The Ministry of Culture was reduced to a secretary," says Cabral. "Progressive programmes are being decimated and thrown out of the door like rubbish. To recover from it, and everything that surrounds this idea, will take a few generations."

Vázquez says: "If we relied on the federal government's political project for culture, we would have only gospel

ABOVE: Rodolfo García Vázquez, left, and Ivam Cabral, founders of the São Paulo-based theatre company Os Satyros, which has performed worldwide in countries such as Germany, Spain, USA, France, Italy and the UK.

shows and movies about the Bible – an extremely reactionary project."

For Alves, the Bolsonaro government's message is clear: "They tell us that what you do is not important."

But in the face of all these obstacles, Brazilian theatre remains defiant.

"We are being questioned," says Cabral. "It's very important that we don't shut up, that we denounce, because the world needs to be reinvented. It is up to us in the theatre to educate the public. Not giving in is essential." ✖

Guilherme Osinski is Tim Hetherington Fellow and editorial assistant at Index on Censorship; Mark Seacombe is associate editor at Index

50(04):84/86|DOI:10.1177/03064220211068710

 'If we relied on federal government, we'd have only gospel shows and Bible movies'

CREDIT: André Stefano

COMMENT

"If the UK is serious about women's rights – and women's rights are human rights – they should follow the European parliament's lead and reconsider whether we want to participate in Expo 2020"

CAITLIN MAY MCNAMARA ON WHY GOVERNMENTS AND COMPANIES SHOULD NOT IGNORE HUMAN
RIGHTS VIOLATIONS | THE WORLD IS APPLAUDING THE MAN WHO ASSAULTED ME, PAGE 97

Elephant that should be in Nobel room

JOHN SWEENEY believes the winners of this year's Peace Prize deserve their accolade, but that there is another who should have taken the award

S AY WHAT YOU like about the master of the Kremlin – that he is a poisoner, a psychopath, a serial killer – Vladimir Vladimirovich Putin does have a sly sense of humour. And so does his right-hand man, Dmitry Peskov.

When the Nobel Peace Prize was co-awarded to a bold and good Russian journalist, Dmitry Muratov, Peskov deadpanned: "We can congratulate Dmitry Muratov. He persistently works in accordance with his own ideals, he is devoted to them, he is talented, he is brave."

When the Kremlin salutes a Nobel Peace Prize winner you sit up and take notice. The elephant not in the room is the man who didn't win the prize, who is not talented, who is not brave, who cannot be named. That is the man who the Kremlin fears, who they tried to kill, who they have now locked up. That elephant is Alexei Navalny who many, including me, think should have won it.

LEFT: Alexei Navalny is rubbed out after a mural appeared overnight in Vladimir Putin's home city of St Petersburg

Maria Ressa is a fighter for human rights, a restless, bubbly, tiny ball of energy exuding a forcefield. I met her at a recent Magnitsky Awards ceremony and came away feeling almost sorry for the Philippines' almost-gangster president, Rodrigo Duterte.

Ressa's journalism has shone a bleak spotlight on Duterte's corrupt and murderous rule and it is largely due to her that, in October, he announced he was leaving politics next year. But the Philippines does not have nuclear weapons and its leader, despite his many faults, is not in effect undermining democracy in the West. Putin is.

Right now, Putin seems to be throttling gas supplies to Europe so that this winter, shivering in the dark, it will give the green light to Nord Stream 2. This gas pipeline bypasses Ukraine, the Czech Republic and so on, making it easier for the Kremlin to bully its old dominions. Unease at Putin's knee being on Europe's gas neck is not diminished by the fact that the man in charge is Matthias Warnig, a former Stasi officer when Putin was a KGB agent in East Germany. Warnig denies this, saying he met Putin only in 1991. Warnig's boss is the former chancellor of Germany, Gerhard Schröder, married five times with no children. Until, that is, Putin gave him two orphans from St Petersburg. There is, of course, no suggestion that Putin, Warnig and Schröder have done anything wrong.

Muratov helped create Novaya Gazeta, what many call the last good newspaper in Russia. When accepting the award, he said exactly the right thing: "It's not mine. I'm not the right beneficiary, there are real ones. It's just that the Nobel Peace Prize isn't awarded posthumously, it's awarded to living people. Obviously, they decided to award it to someone living, having in mind Yuri Shchekochikhin,

Igor Domnikov, Anna Politkovskaya, Anastasia Baburova, Stanislav Markelov, and Natalya Estemirova."

Those six people all worked for Novaya Gazeta. They died in the line of fire.

And Muratov himself thinks that the award went to the wrong man: "If I had been on the Nobel Peace Prize committee, I would have voted for the person whom the bookmakers bet on. I mean Alexei Navalny."

Navalny is locked up in an uber-prison near Vladimir, east of Moscow, for the crime of not honouring his parole while he was in a coma, having been poisoned by the military grade nerve agent, Novichok. Through his lawyers, Navalny congratulated Muratov, reflecting that Novaya Gazeta's six murdered journalists showed "what a high price those who refuse to serve the authorities have to pay".

Writing in The New York Times, Anton Troianovski set out how the Kremlin makes hay with the fault line that runs between journalists such as Muratov, who work inside the system, and people such as Navalny, who make few, if any, compromises.

Troianovski wrote: "Muratov acknowledges that he holds back on what has become a particularly explosive sort of investigative journalism in today's Russia: exploring the hidden wealth of Putin and his inner circle. Muratov says that though his reporters also pursue corruption investigations, 'we don't get into people's private lives. When it comes to children and women — I stop'." →

What makes arguing this point so tricky is that the two joint winners of the prize this year – Muratov and Filipina journalist Maria Ressa – are worthy recipients and morally streets better than some previous winners, such as Nixon apologist Henry Kissinger and Vietnamese Stalinist Le Duc Tho.

When the Kremlin salutes a Nobel Peace Prize winner you sit up and take notice

ABOVE: The Filipina journalist Maria Ressa is 'a worthy recipient of the Nobel Peace Prize and morally streets better than some previous winners, such as the Nixon apologist Henry Kissinger'

→ Others don't. I'm thinking of Roman Badanin, the journalist working for the Proekt website, who reported on the extraordinary wealth of one-time St Petersburg cleaner Svetlana Krivonogikh and her daughter, who is the spitting image of Putin. Badanin's flat in Moscow was raided recently. He has now upped sticks and spends his time in the USA – one of many independent reporters and Navalnyites who have been forced to leave Russia for good in the last 12 months.

There is, of course, no better form of censorship than locking someone up for a crime that does not exist – apart from, that is, the ultimate form of censorship.

Navalny, for the moment, is playing a game of dare with Putin, and he is so obviously Public Enemy Number One of the Kremlin that they dare not kill him. But they can make his life miserable. Recently, the prison authorities deemed him "a terrorist" and he faces a further decade in prison if he is convicted.

Two former convicts in the prison told Dozhd TV that a claque of "trusty"

> There is no better form of censorship than locking someone up for a non-existent crime

inmates were paid 7,000 roubles (about $95) in cash and granted perks to psychologically torture Navalny, dogging his every move. One prisoner urinated on him to provoke Navalny to hit him and on his birthday in June prisoners were shown a short film suggesting he was homosexual – a potentially lethal move among Russia's homophobic prison population.

Prison bosses placed an inmate believed to be suffering from tuberculosis in a bunk close to Navalny and a second inmate was a mentally ill prisoner in the bunk next to him, who "burped, spat and masturbated" throughout the night.

This is an old trick. My late friend Vaughan Barrett – gumshoe reporter for New York's Village Voice – crashed the opening of one of Donald Trump's casinos in Atlantic City in the 1980s. Trump's security was handled by moonlighting Atlantic City police officers and Barrett spent the night in a police cell, chained to a radiator next to a mentally ill man who spent the night masturbating, no doubt dreaming of making America great again.

The Russian prison service has made no comment on the allegations that Navalny is in effect being tortured.

The black spot against Navalny dates back to around 2007 when he drifted to the nationalist right and put up a video condemning immigrants mainly from Russia's (mainly Muslim) south as "cockroaches".

He has since navigated back to the liberal centre, but he has never admitted his mistake. So did the Nobel people dis Navalny because he might have been a racist?

Marvin Rees is the black mayor of Bristol, in the UK, who spent a term at Yale on its World Fellows programme and his mate was Navalny. Rees told me: "When I first got there, I didn't have a car. Alexei offered to take me to a supermarket, sat outside waiting while I got my supplies." Later, the two families went apple picking together. "In terms of the charge of being racist, I take someone as I find them. I didn't meet someone who approached me with any sort of hate or hostility. I met someone who treated me with respect, treated me as a friend."

So did the Nobel Peace Prize committee make a big mistake by not honouring Navalny?

(By the way, the Nobel prizes were set up thanks only to a cock-up. In 1888, the death of Ludvig Nobel caused several papers to publish obituaries of his brother, Alfred. One French newspaper wrote: "The merchant of death is dead… Dr Alfred Nobel, who became rich by finding ways to kill more people faster than ever before, died yesterday." Alfred was very much

The charge against the Nobel nabobs is that they were worried about taking a risk

alive, and upset. His great invention, dynamite, was an explosive used in civilian life, not a military weapon. To ensure his legacy, he set up the prizes in his name.)

The charge against the Nobel Prize nabobs is that they are comfortable people living comfortable lives who were worried about taking a reputational risk

on Navalny – and, in ducking the big decision, delighted the Kremlin.

Once again, I admire Ressa and Muratov very much, but right now Putin is riding high. The USA and Europe are divided and democracy is in the doldrums while the authoritarian powers are doing very nicely, thank you.

The one person who counters that narrative is sitting in a prison cell, alone and abused. And on those grounds alone, the prisoner of the Kremlin gets my vote. ✖

John Sweeney is a writer and journalist who has investigated Scientology and Russian interference in the US elections. He is the host of the Hunting Ghislaine podcast

50(04):88/91|DOI:10.1177/03064220211068711

RIGHT: Prizewinner Dmitry Muratov helped create Novaya Gazeta, what many call the last good newspaper in Russia

We academics must fight the mob – now

The appalling hounding of Kathleen Stock at the University of Sussex is a serious threat to freedom of speech on campus, argues **ARIF AHMED**

FREE SPEECH MATTERS everywhere and always; but for at least two reasons universities have a special duty to protect it for students and staff.

The first is that most students attend university at a formative time – between school and working life. Their opinions are not yet settled; and once embarked on work it is much harder to take a step back and think about what you really care about, what sort of person you are, or what you want from life. That self-discovery can only be pursued by exploring many options – intellectual, political, sexual, or whatever it may be – and this exploration is only possible when there is no pressure to conform to any orthodoxy. Academic freedom is a prerequisite for the academy as a place of self-discovery.

The second reason is that universities are where experts in their fields – in family law or epigraphy or cosmology or logic – engage in research, which often means disputes, that advance knowledge and can contribute to public discourse. It is a comforting fiction that progress – including moral progress – is always collaborative. Real progress demands a refining process; and that in turn means the freedom to be frank in ways that are often uncomfortable.

Both reasons apply when we consider intellectual debates that connect deeper questions of individual identity with questions in public policy. The issues raised by the government's 2018 public consultation on the Gender Recognition Act 2004 (GRA) are examples of that.

The Act itself had allowed people – for instance, those with gender dysphoria – to apply for a certificate confirming a new gender; for most purposes the possessor of such a Gender Recognition Certificate (GRC) would then be legally recognised as being of the new gender. The new consultation was (among other things) over whether to relax the conditions under which a person could obtain a GRC. Would it be necessary to have a medical diagnosis of gender dysphoria to receive such a certificate?

On the one hand, the question raises philosophical matters to do with whether and how gender is a social construction, also over its connection with identity and its connection with biological sex. On the other hand, it raised public policy questions to do with the segregation of access to facilities: how stringent should the conditions be under which, for instance, someone born as a man could obtain a certificate entitling them to use women's lavatories, take part in women's sports, and so on?

Here then, freedom of speech in an academic context is obviously important. It matters that people feel free to argue both for and against relaxing the requirements for a GRC. Indeed that is what should happen; but it is not happening. The Sussex philosopher Kathleen Stock began writing about the GRA in 2018, in academic journals but also on blogs, in comment pieces for the press and so on. She argued (among other things) that there were costs, to people born women, of expanding the category of "woman" to include anyone who calls themselves one. Because of her intervention, Professor Stock has been subject to a sustained campaign of vilification and harassment.

Stock's case is unusual by historical standards. In the past, perhaps even today, the principal threat to academic freedom came from the authorities (state or university). In 1687 James II tried to expel the Fellows of Magdalen College, Oxford, who had resisted his favoured choice for president of that institution; the attempt failed and was one of

Hundreds of academics have complained about having to walk on eggshells over gender, sex and transsexuality

ABOVE: Transgender people and supporters protest in Parliament Square, London

several disasters that together fatally undermined him.

The threat from authority has hardly gone away. In 2021 Abertay University, in Dundee, began disciplinary hearings against a student who had dared to say that women have vaginas; again, the attempt failed, though as far as I know nobody at Abertay has suffered the fate of the last Stuart monarch.

In Stock's case though, it was not the state that attacked her; and the university authorities supported her – or, at least, they supported her in the latest, most serious round of protests, having failed to do so previously. But she was subject to abuse and harassment by individuals. Sussex admitted as much in October 2021, though by then police had advised her to avoid her place of work, to employ a bodyguard if she ventured on to campus and to install CCTV outside her home, so it was hardly being controversial. In any case,

the upshot was that Stock left her job and in November became a Founding Fellow of the new University of Austin in Texas. The UK regulator of Higher Education, the Office for Students, has now launched an investigation into whether the University of Sussex has "met its obligations for academic freedom and freedom of speech within the law for all students and staff, whatever their views".

Without anticipating what that inquiry finds, it is possible to make two points about this deeply concerning case.

The first is that in principle there may be academic freedom issues on both sides: one side points, rightly, to Stock's right to lecture, write and speak without fear of harassment; the other side points, again rightly, to the right of students (or anyone else) to protest against her. But

we must distinguish peaceful protest in favour of a principle like rights for trans people – which, incidentally, Stock has publicly defended – and harassment and victimisation of an individual aimed at blocking their speech (or worse). It seems that both things were happening at Sussex; but while the former is defensible on free speech grounds, the latter certainly is not.

Second, Stock's case is extreme but far from unique. In one recent case more than 500 students petitioned Oxford University to force two professors to include trans women in their research into women's equality, so as not to create a "hostile and exclusionary atmosphere". One of those professors, Selina Todd, had to be accompanied to lectures by security guards because of credible threats to her physical safety. Professor Jo Phoenix and Professor Rosa Freedman had talks cancelled at Essex University after they were accused of transphobia; an 18-month independent inquiry by a barrister concluded that Essex had failed to uphold free speech.

And these are just the highlights, if that is the word, of a pervasive phenomenon. Hundreds of academics across the UK have written, anonymously, about having to walk on eggshells when it comes to issues around gender, sex and transsexuality.

All this points to something much worse than Stock's harassment, appalling though that is: the wholesale censorship, by a mob, of a legitimate and important point of view on a matter of public interest. We – I mean we academics – must fight back now; unless we do so, I fear people will look back at 2021 as the time that we let free speech die. ✖

Arif Ahmed, a philosopher and a Fellow of Gonville and Caius College, Cambridge, was given the Index on Censorship trustees' award in 2021 for championing free speech on campus

50(04):92/93|DOI:10.1177/03064220211068712

So who is judging YouTube?

Accused by the video behemoth of spreading misinformation, **KEITH KAHN-HARRIS** conducted an experiment in an effort to understand how the social media platform polices its content

T'S NOT EVERY day that I am accused of spreading falsehoods, so I was shocked to receive an email from YouTube in October 2021 that began:

We wanted to let you know our team reviewed your content, and we think it violates our medical misinformation policy.

The email said that, although my channel wouldn't be removed, one of the videos I had uploaded had been taken down. Still, there were words of comfort:

We realise this may be disappointing news, but it's our job to make sure that YouTube is a safe place for all. If you think we've made a mistake, you can appeal this decision.

I did appeal; immediately and in the most emphatic terms. A few hours later I received notice that my appeal had been turned down and that "we won't be putting your content back up on YouTube". No further appeals allowed.

So what misinformation had I spread?

You can see for yourself – the video is also hosted on Vimeo and remains online at **vimeo.com/288339463**. It's a trailer that my publishers produced for my book Denial: The Unspeakable Truth when it came out in 2018.

I had uploaded it to YouTube and it never attracted more than a few hundred views during the three years it was up.

The book dissects a range of "denialisms" (including anti-vaxxing), assesses the future of the phenomenon and speculates on what it would take to make denialism history. As the rapid

growth in medical misinformation during the Covid pandemic has shown, the book didn't stop this phenomenon.

Still, YouTube wasn't making a judgment on the effectiveness of my arguments but on the content of the video. So what did it find so objectionable?

I don't know for sure: the email contained no specific information on what the problem was or how the assessment was made. There are a couple of things that might have raised some flags. One was that the voiceover was compiled from a cacophony of voices of denialists themselves – including ones disparaging accepted scholarship on vaccines, Aids, the Holocaust, climate change. The other is that the blurb was taken from the publisher's website, which begins:

The Holocaust never happened. The planet isn't warming. Vaccines cause autism. There is no such thing as Aids. The Earth is flat.

So it seems that quotation of medical misinformation – in the second instance, ironic quotation – triggered YouTube's disciplinary process. Whether it was quotation in the video itself, in the blurb or both remains unclear.

I also don't know who or what made this judgment. Was it one of those fabled algorithms? Or a

(probably underpaid and undertrained) worker making dozens of such decisions every day? Or was the judgment made by a member of the public who reported the video (maybe maliciously)? And was the appeal handled by a human or an algorithm?

Either way, the thing or person making the decisions could not distinguish between quotation/irony and serious intent.

This is a bizarre kind of Turing Test: is YouTube's incompetence down to an incompetent human or an incompetent algorithm?

The information on the YouTube website does not help clarify matters. The page titled "How does YouTube manage harmful content?" states:

We remove content that violates our policies as quickly as possible, using a combination of people and machine learning to detect potentially problematic content on a massive scale. In addition, we rely on the YouTube community as well as experts in our Trusted Flagger programme to help us spot potentially problematic content by reporting it directly to us. We also go to great lengths to make sure that content that violates our policies isn't widely viewed, or even viewed at all, before →

 What I am not sympathetic to is the persistent denial by social media companies about who they actually are. Whether they want to be or not, they are publishers

'Kafkaesque' is a misused term, but for social media companies it seems justified

→ *it's removed. Our automated flagging systems help us detect and review content even before it's seen by our community. Once such content is identified, human content reviewers evaluate whether it violates our policies. If it does, we remove the content and use it to train our machines for better coverage in the future. Our content reviewers also protect content that has a clear educational, documentary, scientific or artistic [EDSA] purpose.*

Such generalities do not help in isolating where the process broke down here.

I am not the first person to be mystified by the capricious application of YouTube's takedown policy (or, indeed, those of other social networks). In January 2021, talkRADIO's channel was taken down for "violating YouTube's community guidelines". Although YouTube confirmed that some content appeared to violate Covid-19 guidance, the entire channel was restored within a day. At the end of October, the entire channel of the left-wing news website Novara Media was taken down for about two hours. On that occasion, it appeared that some of the channel's content had been flagged by members of the public (who can report violations of YouTube guidelines), and on review it was reinstated.

In order to try to penetrate the mystery of YouTube's decision-making process, I decided to conduct an experiment. While I might not be able to discover who or what made the call in my case, I could at least identify whether it was the video or the blurb or both that brought down its wrath.

I created a new YouTube account in a false name and recorded two very short videos. One of them featured a statement that vaccines, including the Covid vaccine, were dangerous and no one should take them. The other featured a statement proclaiming the exact opposite.

I titled them "Vaccines are great! Everyone should take the Covid vaccine!" and "Vaccines are dangerous! No one should take the Covid vaccine!"

The twist was that I applied the title to the wrong videos – so the anti-vax video had a pro-vaccine title and vice versa. That way, if one were taken down and the other stayed online, I'd be able to tell what aspect of the content infringed YouTube's policies.

Within half a day of posting, one of them had indeed been taken down: "Vaccines are great! Everyone should take the Covid vaccine!" The one with the anti-vax title, though, remains online at the time of writing, nearly a week after posting.

You can view the videos (now safely, for the moment, archived on Vimeo at **vimeo.com/641997900**). It seems that the video content itself was what breached YouTube's rules. At least in my experiment, the title seemed to make no difference. Or did it? Perhaps in this case the irony of the titles was recognised and the content made no difference.

Actually, my experiment may have made YouTube's policies and processes less clear. And that's the point: they constitute a "black box" to which we have no access and, even if the processes are rigorous and consistent, they seem capricious and incoherent. As in all cases of judgment and disciplining, only full transparency can reassure those being judged that the system is fair.

In the interest of encouraging that transparency, I contacted YouTube's press office to explain what I had done and share an early draft of this article.

At the time of writing, there has been no response. While in high-profile cases such as Novara Media and talkRADIO, YouTube have issued statements (albeit not very helpful ones), for minnows like me it is almost impossible to engage the company in any kind of dialogue.

I have a lot of sympathy for these companies in that I can appreciate how hard it is to monitor the vast amount of information posted online every second. And it's likely that quotation, irony and sarcasm constitute a massive challenge in content monitoring.

Even though companies such as Google, which owns YouTube, are almost inconceivably wealthy, the employment and training of sufficient numbers of staff capable of executing fine and nuanced judgments in a consistent way might burn through even their vast profits.

What I am not sympathetic to is the persistent denial by social media companies about who they actually are. Whether they want to be or not, they are publishers and ultimately responsible for the content they produce. Whether they want to be or not, some of them have become de facto public utilities, from whom exclusion is such a weighty matter that it requires the same accountability and transparency as exclusion from any other public good demands.

"Kafkaesque" is a much misused term, but applying it to social media companies seems justified. In The Trial, Kafka described the disorientation produced by a justice system whose inner workings were mysterious. Treating YouTube et al as if they were the organs of a state might force them to acknowledge their power and to accept the responsibilities that go with it. ✖

Keith Kahn-Harris is a sociologist and writer. His latest book is The Babel Message: A Love Letter to Language (Icon)

50(04):94/96|DOI:10.1177/03064220211068714

Why is the world applauding the man who assaulted me?

CAITLIN MAY MCNAMARA, who was sexually assaulted in Abu Dhabi, says it's time for governments and businesses to decide where their priorities lie

PICTURED: 'I learned the hard way,' says McNamara

EXPO 2020 IN Dubai is the first Expo in the Middle East and 192 countries have come together with international organisations, businesses and educational institutions for a six-month showcase of innovation and ideas – a year later than planned, due to Covid-19 – under the theme of "Connecting Minds, Creating the Future".

But this is not a future that is safe for women.

Last year, I was sexually assaulted by the commissioner-general of the Dubai Expo, Sheikh Nahyan bin Mubarak al-Nahyan during a meeting in Abu Dhabi, and despite UK authorities acknowledging that there was enough evidence of rape to prosecute if the attack had happened in Britain, there was no jurisdiction to proceed – and the UAE has done nothing to prosecute him or prevent it from happening to others. [Following publication of the allegations in The Sunday Times, law firm Schillings responded on behalf of Sheikh Nahyan as follows: "Our client is surprised and saddened by this allegation, which arrives eight months after the alleged incident and via a national newspaper. The account is denied."]

In December 2021, I watched him being applauded on stage when he delivered a speech at the Women's Pavilion, an Expo platform dedicated to the idea "that when women thrive, humanity thrives". His unelected power and financial privilege allow him to continue in the international limelight with impunity.

While the Expo's PR experts are busy presenting an image of women's empowerment, evidence came before a UK parliamentary panel in November that revealed a different story.

Their fact-finding report included the story of another British woman, a professional with two young children who remained anonymous to the panel for safety reasons, who was arbitrarily detained for 18 months recently. She was denied the right to a fair trial, with most of her hearings taking place in →

LEFT: Fashion brand Cartier is the partner of Expo 2020's Women's Pavilion

→ Arabic, and denied direct access to legal representation. She was allowed to see her children only once in those 18 months, and for just 25 minutes.

The Alternative Human Rights Expo, a campaign of more than 20 rights groups, has been dedicated to countering the glimmering narrative of the Dubai Expo's spin by highlighting the repression still happening in the country.

Emirati laws fail to criminalise marital rape, as well as "chastisement" in the form of physical violence by a husband. Laws also still give male guardians authority over women and loopholes allow reduced sentences for men who kill female relatives.

On a day-to-day level, freedom of expression appears to be a luxury not afforded to women in the UAE. Peaceful activists such as Maryam al-Balushi, Amina al-Alabdouli and Ali Abdulnour have been detained and tortured for speaking out. Abdulnour eventually died in custody, while a prominent UAE activist, Alaa al-Siddiq, was subjected to an intense government-requested surveillance campaign via the controversial Israeli technology firm NSO before her death in the UK this summer in a car accident.

The experiences of Dubai princesses Shamsa, Haya and Latifa, who have either disappeared from public view or been targeted after falling out with Dubai's ruler Sheikh Mohammed bin Rashid al-Maktoum, show that even the most progressive of the Emirates' rulers remain oppressive in their own households and women cannot count on state-led reforms to protect them. If seemingly privileged women are treated that badly, what chance do other women there have?

The UAE likes to remind its critics about recent reforms such as the amendment to laws allowing unmarried couples to cohabit and criminalising so-called "honour killings". A requirement under the Personal Status Law for women to be "obedient" to their husbands has also been revoked.

The country has also ratified an updated Federal Crime and Punishment Law, which promises enhanced protections for women, which is due to take effect on 2 January 2022.

Experiences like mine have focused international attention on the UAE. These efforts are a step in the right direction but do not go anywhere near dismantling the deep discrimination against women both in UAE law and in social and government attitudes, especially when it comes to the interests of the rich and powerful. It also remains to be seen whether the new laws will apply to the UAE's ruling families and their entourages.

After I was assaulted in Abu Dhabi, my instinct was to report what had happened to the police. However, everyone I turned to for help reminded me of my attacker's royal status and the threat of the UAE's medieval extramarital sex laws, which load rape survivors with the risk of imprisonment. Finally, the British consulate's legal counsel cut to the chase, telling me that no one inside the UAE would be able to take on a case against al-Nahyan in an independent way. I was advised to leave the country immediately for my safety.

These reforms are nothing more than a sham if they don't treat the rich and powerful as they routinely treat poor black and brown people.

I suspect that the outcome to my case would have been very different had the sexual violence I survived occurred at the hands of the Filipino man who cleaned my room instead of a royal. But some rapes are considered more important than others.

These reforms too often exclude the rights of domestic workers, many of whom are women from India and south-east Asia.

Gaping holes in gender-based violence laws such as this are of particular concern, while international law remains unfit for purpose to protect women, epitomising how our rights are susceptible to neglect globally. The UAE is by no means alone in using high-profile events such as Expo to court

Freedom of expression appears to be a luxury not afforded to women in the UAE

CREDIT: (left) Expo 2020 ; (right) Alexander Astafyev/POOL/TASS/Alamy

international validation while disguising its human rights record. There has long been a strain in the Gulf between countries' human rights records and the international cultural and sports events held there.

What is perhaps more shocking is how easily the UK government, businesses and tourism are willing to turn a blind eye if it serves their financial interests.

As I awaited the UK's Crown Prosecution Service verdict in my case, a couple of miles away from my flat the UK Prime Minister Boris Johnson hosted three other al-Nahyans, negotiating a £10 billion trade deal, which his country is more reliant on than ever post-Brexit.

Afterwards, his office released a statement to say that Johnson was looking forward to the Dubai Expo.

In November, as Iranian delegates were being wined and dined at COP26 in Scotland, Richard Ratcliffe sat outside the UK's Foreign Office at the end of his three-week hunger strike, which was a desperate plea for help to secure the release of his wife, Nazanin Zaghari-Ratcliffe, who has been arbitrarily detained in Iran for more than five years.

Sports stars, brands, tourists and entertainers flocked to be part of lucrative contracts in the Saudi Arabian motor-racing Grand Prix in December, helping to restore the reputation of a regime that puts women's rights activists on trial and kills its critics. Football fans will do the same at Qatar's 2022 World Cup next year, with little thought to the human cost of the migrant workers who have been building their stadiums.

When I was first approached to work in the UAE, I was hesitant. I had specialised in cultural diplomacy since studying politics at university, and collaborated with arts, media and human rights organisations across the Arab world in the decade since.

I was aware of the moral predicament of working on a platform of free expression in a country that regularly locks up prisoners of conscience and had no desire to be a

These reforms are nothing more than a sham if they don't treat the rich and powerful as they routinely treat poor black and brown people

pawn in an Emirati PR stunt.

However, I believed that engagement was a more productive means of moving forward than boycotting and that a British cultural organisation crying "boycott" over engaging with a country that invests in its arts sector would be short-sighted.

My view has changed. Learning the hard way that the law does not protect me in the UAE, the beliefs that I previously lived by have lost their shine.

In October 2021, the European Parliament passed a resolution that cited my case, advising EU member states to boycott the Dubai Expo in disapproval of UAE's human rights record.

ABOVE: Sheikh Nahyan bin Mubarak al-Nahyan: "His unelected power and financial privilege allow him to continue in the international limelight with impunity," says McNamara

If the UK is serious about women's rights – and women's rights are human rights – it should follow the European Parliament's lead and reconsider whether we want to participate in an event and, in doing so, legitimise a country that has such poor justice provisions for women.

Expo 2020 aims to attract a total of 25 million visitors. But without adequate justice provisions for women, these visitors are not safe.

During my six-month stay in the UAE, I was struck by the warm hospitality and humour of the Emirati community that I was working with and the sense of possibility and optimism that felt stark in contrast to the UK. I met people and organisations doing formidable work and who were courteous and collaborative enough to request the engagement and approval of the international community.

Yet the country is impoverished by leaders and institutions who treat women, girls and other marginalised communities – migrant workers, Yemeni civilians, those without means and privilege – as disposable objects devoid of human rights.

Expo 2020 Dubai presents an uncomfortable but deeply important choice for business and government leaders: stand with women or stand with those who wish to silence us by any means necessary.

Please choose wisely. ✖

Caitlin May McNamara is a journalist and campaigner living in London. In 2019, she was recruited to lead Hay Festival's inaugural edition in Abu Dhabi.

50(04):97/99|DOI:10.1177/03064220211068715

GLOBAL VIEW

Silence is not golden

As we enter a new year, Index will continue to act as a voice for those unable to use their own, says **RUTH SMEETH**

THIS YEAR HAS been a rollercoaster. In the shadow of Covid-19 the focus of every country retreated to their own streets. Public health has understandably dominated the news agenda as more than 264 million of us have been infected by a disease unheard of two years ago, with over five million of our friends and family now taken by it.

These numbers are almost impossible to comprehend and our thoughts, daily, are with those who are grieving and those who are struggling to recover from this horrible virus.

But as we emerge from the pandemic, we must start to consider what the additional human costs of being distracted have been. The impact of our leaders going missing in action from the global stage and if not missing then impotent to the challenges undermining our rules-based world order.

> ## In response to world events 2021, the year we turned 50, has been one of our busiest

The year started with the storming of the US Capitol on 6 January and the bad news seemed to follow from there. We have seen the collapse of Afghanistan. The failure of COP26 to agree the end of the use of fossil fuels. The arrests of nearly every democracy campaigner in Hong Kong. A military coup in Myanmar. A resurgent Putin and an intransigent Lukashenka – two tyrants who have sought to destabilise and potentially bring the world towards renewed conflict in Europe. And these are just the top lines – in every corner of the planet repressive governments are seeking to silence their populations – to restrict freedoms guaranteed by the Universal Declaration of Human Rights.

Every assault on democracy has undermined our collective fundamental freedom of free expression. Each conflict has, by default, silenced the voices of dissidents, curtailed their art, their journalism and their creativity. To challenge the efforts of tyrants to make the world grey is the reason why Index was founded and why we're still here.

In response to world events 2021, the year we turned 50, has been one of our busiest. We've rebranded as an organisation and redesigned the magazine. We've launched projects and worked with new correspondents worldwide. We've commissioned artwork and supported Freedom of Expression Award winners. And we've launched legal challenges in the UK and supported others further afield to ensure legal protections of freedom of expression.

But it's not the issues that we have covered that keep me awake (well only occasionally). It's the fear of what we're missing – of who we aren't helping. Of where we aren't able to shine a spotlight.

It is the thought of the political prisoners whose voices have been silenced as hundreds of thousands have been detained. It is the women who aren't allowed to work or drive or walk without a man being present – never mind draw or write. It is the young people who are exploring their

ABOVE: Women in some countries cannot work or drive without a man present

sexuality in places where homosexuality is banned. The minority communities whose voices are considered too revolutionary to be heard. It is the young person whose community is being destroyed by war, or famine, or flood.

Index was established as a vehicle of solidarity. To provide hope to those losing faith that the world could know of their plight. This is our mission, these people are our priority, and this is what we must strive to do day in, day out.

As we enter 2022 our relentless focus will be on providing a voice for the persecuted. But this doesn't mean that we won't be fighting to protect the principles of free expression at home too. Whether that's our rights online, on campus or in law. Index will be a bastion against any and all attacks on our rights to free speech.

But none of this work can be achieved without your support and that of our funders. We are a voice for the persecuted – because of you. Thank you

Season's greetings and hope for a more collaborative and positive 2022. ✖

Ruth Smeeth is CEO of Index on Censorship

50(04):100/100|DOI:10.1177/03064220211068716

CULTURE

"Those who are squeamish about mud wouldn't set foot here.
And yet Angelina Jolie has been here.
Aung San Suu Kyi has been here."

THITSAR NI, PICTURED IN HIS HOME IN MYANMAR, IS AMONG THE POETS WHOSE WORK WAS PERFORMED
DURING BANNED BOOKS WEEK | BEARING WITNESS THROUGH POETRY, PAGE 104

The road of no return

The Uyghur activist and poet Aziz Isa Elkun, exiled in the UK, yearns for his family and friends imprisoned in Chinese concentration camps. He talks to **FLO MARKS**

THE POEM ROSES is dedicated to the Uyghurs arrested and detained in the Chinese Communist Party's 21st-century concentration camps in what is officially called the Xinjiang Uyghur Autonomous Region.

Its author, Uyghur poet, writer and academic Aziz Isa Elkun, grew up in Shahyar county, close to the Tarim river, and did not experience the freedom promised in the region's colonial name.

Now 51, he was first arrested as a 16-year-old schoolboy in 1986 when his activism led to him being informally detained and interrogated. His home was ransacked and his earliest journals taken away. He was released after two days, but his parents' defence of young naivety was unlikely to save him from a prison sentence in the future.

As the political climate worsened, with increasing government surveillance and censorship, it became increasingly certain that Aziz, as a young adult who favoured

freedom of expression and association, would keep getting into trouble.

His commitment to these ideals was cemented when he took part in the student movement in Urumqi.

The frequent investigations, the threats of imprisonment and his unemployment gave him the impetus to flee the mainland, travelling first to Central Asia, in 1999, and then to Germany, before reaching the UK in 2001.

Deciding to become an active member of the diaspora was never free of consequences. Despite living in exile for more than 20 years, Aziz told Index he had never once "stopped worrying" about his friends, family and homeland who he left behind "and remain at the

whim of China's primitive and feudal revenge system", potentially being punished for his activist work abroad.

In 2017, he learned that his sister and cousins had been imprisoned in the camps. He found the grave of his father, who died of natural causes, on Google Maps – but this was later demolished in a wave of cultural genocide.

With communication cut off, he now has no way of knowing the fate of his mother. But he said: "I am a conscious and free human and British citizen. It's my basic

 After 20 years away, he has never stopped worrying about those he left behind

Roses

By **AZIZ ISA ELKUN**

It's a morning bright with sun
Another new day has started
I count, altogether twenty-two autumns
And winters have passed in exile
And I don't know how many years remain
Before I return to the place where I belong
To the earth that my forefathers made home.

I can feel the sorrow in myself.
My soul shivers; it's cold
I inherited it all from my father
Whenever the memory of the disappeared homeland
Returns and occupies my mind
It inspires me to be human with dignity
Able to call for the survival of a lost nation
Able to appeal for mercy and love
From the world
Again and again.

The place where I was born
Has turned into a heap of ghostly relics
It only exists amongst the non-existence
In this world full of selfishness.

I am sitting in a garden chair
Trying to enjoy the warm sun for a minute
But it is quickly covered by the rushing clouds
A steaming cup of coffee evaporates my gloom
I am still struggling to feel myself
Believing that better days will come after tomorrow.

One day life will smile on us
Even on the man who writes these lines
Although he lost everything
Travelling on the road of no return
And lived a second life
He is still a hostage to that place
He lives with constant fear

The monster has left countless stains
It has pierced me with needles
But still I call for justice for those
Who have suffered more
But my spirit is still fighting
My hope is still alive
Each time I find new courage
It brings the joy of a smile

Although it's autumn
My garden leaves are still green
The first rose I planted three years ago
To mark my father's destroyed grave
The second rose I planted
On Mother's Day last year
The third rose I planted for the unknown Uyghurs
Who survive inside the camps

My roses are blossoming with hope
Singing a song of freedom
Without waiting for the spring
They remind us
How beautiful it is to be alive
To live in peace in our beautiful world.

10 October 2021, London

right to exercise freedom of expression and protest; it's not up to China."

Having previously used only a typewriter, learning English and modern technology gave Aziz an unprecedented sense of freedom akin to being "reborn". Yet it simultaneously brought awareness of the extent of censorship and false information surrounding the Uyghurs.

Feeling it was his calling to debunk the pervasive myth that Uyghurs were a happy minority under the CCP, he has set up 10 websites and platforms and is the director of the Uyghur PEN Revitalisation Project. Written in English and the all-too-rare Uyghur script, these projects aim to share reputable work and information to reach, connect and promote the visibility of the diaspora. This is because, when faced with genocide, he values improving understanding of Uyghur identity, culture, history and current travails as a vital act of resistance and solidarity. ✖

Flo Marks is a researcher at Index on Censorship and a Students for Uyghurs Ambassador at the University of Exeter

50(04):102/103|DOI:10.1177/03064220211068717

Bearing witness through poetry

Two writers on the frontline of censorship share their stories with **EMMA SANDVIK LING**

MARKING BANNED BOOKS Week 2021, Index on Censorship and the British Library hosted an online conversation and recital with Myanmar's ko ko thett and Kurdish poet, writer and academic Choman Hardi, chaired by the deputy chair of Index on Censorship's board of trustees, Kate Maltby. The speakers reflected on their personal experiences with poetry, protest and censorship.

Banned Books Week was first held in 1982 in reaction to a surge in the number of challenges to books in the USA. But banning books is still prevalent today. In November 2021 the Spotsylvania County Public School Board ordered school libraries to remove "sexually explicit" literature. Defending the decision, a board member, Kirk Twigg, said he wanted to "see the books before we burn them so we can identify within our community that we are eradicating this bad stuff". Similar incidents have been happening across the country.

While incitement to burn books paints a dramatic picture, the censorship of literature is often more subtle. Censorship happens when writers are systematically unable to publish their stories, when content is removed from social media, or when writers choose to self-censor because they fear persecution.

ABOVE: The poet Thitsar Ni surrounded by books at his home in Myanmar

Throughout the world, writers face censorship. Both thett and Hardi know this all too well. To mark the 39th annual Banned Books Week, Index on Censorship and the British Library took a closer look at the role of poetry in protest. As thett pointed out, poetry is accessible in a society where resources and free speech are hard to come by: "If you chose to paint or if you chose to do any other thing in art, you need accessories like paint and paint brushes. For poetry you don't even need paper or

a pen if you are a spoken word poet."

Thett jokes that his career was "discreetly launched". He originally published poems in small pamphlets distributed by hand through a network of sympathetic poets and students. Poets were unable to hold public recitals, but would gather in each other's homes for private, secret events. Luckily he was not caught for this although legal issues, including arrests, would come later.

Thett makes a distinction between protest poetry and witness poetry. The former, for him, assumes a political agenda. Witness poetry is a more inclusive term. The poet becomes an observer rather than a political actor.

CREDIT: Craig Ritchie

The poems tell stories of individuals experiencing conflict first hand

In each poem, the poet/researcher asks a survivor to tell her story. Reflecting on the experience of writing the poems, she said: "Every time they cried I cried, and every story in its own way became a nightmare."

Hardi has her own story to tell from the conflict. She was born in Iraq but her family fled to the UK through Iran in the early 1990s. Shei came from a strong literary background and is the youngest child of the Kurdish poet Ahmad Hardi. She reminisced that when they came to England as refugees in 1993, her father lost his social status. In Iraq he was considered a cultural treasure. In England he didn't even speak the language. Poetry became a way for her to tell her own stories and find belonging in a foreign country.

Banned Books Week is a celebration of silenced writers as well as a protest against the censorship of literature. Both thett and Hardi have had personal experiences with persecution and censorship. Likewise, they have both chosen to dedicate their work to giving voices to those who are unable to speak. Their poetry forces the reader to confront difficult emotions. The reader has no choice but to delve into the world of the narrator. This is the radical power of poetry in protest. Thett summarises the importance of their work perfectly. "Writing," he says, "is a form of protest." ✖

Emma Sandvik Ling is events and partnerships manager at Index. She has an MA in international peace and security from King's College London ➜

50(04):104/107|DOI:10.1177/03064220211068739

With this in mind, he is now editing, with Brian Haman, a collection of witness poetry, to be published by Ethos Books in the spring of 2022 (Picking Off New Shoots Will Not Stop the Spring: Witness Poems and Essays from Myanmar, 1988-2021). The collection is of pieces written during the protests in Myanmar as they unfolded over the past year. They tell the stories of individuals experiencing the conflict first-hand and invite audiences to bear witness. On 14 March 2021, at least 39 people were killed in protests in Hlaingthaya township, Myanmar. The poem Hlaingthaya, by Thitsar Ni, which bears witness to that, is published overleaf.

While Choman Hardi's writing comes out of a very different context, her work certainly falls within thett's definition of witness poetry. Her poetry often supplements her academic work, which uses an intersectional lens to examine the experiences of women in war and conflict. Her poetry collection Considering the Women (2015) was inspired by interviews she conducted as part of her post-doctoral research with survivors of the Anfal genocide of Kurds by Saddam Hussein in the late 1980s. She wanted to understand the women's experiences because their stories were often neglected in the media, in academia and in literature.

PICTURED: The city of Yangon, in Myanmar, erupted with protests against the military coup in March 2021

Hlaingthaya

By Thitsar Ni

Up against the metropolitan Yangon
Hlaingthaya is wilderness,
for apoetical Tarzans.
This is where the Irrawaddy delta hobos,
who didn't witness the World Wars
but pushed through the Cyclone Nargis, and the Anyar Mongols,
who left their farms for factories, mingle.
Myanmar's New England doesn't reek of butter.
They don't need a five-star hotel here.
There's Mee-kwet wet market for vegetables.
The place is as plain as instant tea without cream.
The durian husk is known for spikes,
the township is known for hooligans.
At times, it will wash its misdeeds down
in labour protests.
On the Hlaingthaya special menu are
slums and sweat beads,
meagre meals and moonshine stench,

factory smoke and melees.
Those who are squeamish about mud
wouldn't set foot here.
And yet Angelina Jolie has been here.
Aung San Suu Kyi has been here.
In the Spring Revolution
women of this town get obscene
at the Senior General,
men brandish sticks and dahs,
children and grown-ups come together,
"Repress us, we will rise again.
Touch us, we will strike back!"
The curtain to the first defensive war is lifted.
The ideology of the people who haven't got
their nose into "surplus value theory" is
we-have-nothin'-to-lose-ism;
they spit it out like quid betel.
Had only a superior power had to prevail
David would have never beaten Goliath.
A revolution without the precariat is a wingless bird.
A poster reads, "If I am cut down,
the man behind me will cut you down."
Black flags have been raised

on the side of righteousness.
In this sapped spring of endless legends
they will thrive like a flower jungle.
Death is no stranger —
if you daren't fall, you are no flower.

The Angry Survivor

By Choman Hardi

I am fed up with documentations of my grief –
journalists asking me to sing a lullaby for my
dead children, to broadcast during commemorations,
government officials using my story as propaganda
during elections, women activists forcing me to talk
about rape only to prove that women are oppressed,
researchers claiming to record history when
all they do is pick my wounds.

This is my story, not yours. Long after you
turn off your recorder I stay indoors and weep.
Why don't people understand? I am neither hero,
nor God, cannot stand the talk of forgiveness.
For years I went to every wake. Wept at every man's
funeral. Kept asking: Why? Realised I will never
understand. Now I just endure the days, by planting
cucumbers which you interrupted, by believing

in another world where there is justice, by watching my
remaining children as they sleep. Spare me your despair
and understanding. You can't resurrect the dead, feed
my hungry children, bring me recognition and respect.
Take history with you and go. Don't come here
again, I just don't want to know.

His boots

By Choman Hardi

The old woman will always keep those boots.
On the day when things were ending
she was leaning on her stick, in disbelief,

when a car with black windows slowed down.

She watched the back window open fast,
and there he was, the dictator,
suddenly looking old and frail,
dropping his military boots,
replacing them with old men's shoes.

Then the window closed and the car took off,
leaving dust on the pair of boots,
still warm and moist from his feet.

The Seventh Wedding Invitation

By Choman Hardi

Dear friends and family,
I promise this will be my last wedding
if it doesn't work out, I will just live with
another man, no more pledges.
So please come along to this final ceremony with a man
who, at the moment, fills my eyes.
Do not bring any more presents – pura Shahla's
non-stick pan is still in the box. Mama Hama's
gold ring has not been put on. And the naughty
lingerie will be worn for this man since my ex
was orthodox, he didn't last long. Do come along.
I promise to wear something more sophisticated
than a wedding dress. It is another chance to meet
and talk about Ama's failure in bringing up
her children, to shed light, one more time,
on Layla's divorce, and Nina's remarriage
to her brother in law. We will have a fun night.
I have told my new man so much about you
and it may be your only chance to meet him.
With all my love, your little Lala. ✖

Thitsar Ni has published more than 30 books – from poems, essays, short stories and literary critiques to a dictionary of world politics. Choman Hardi is an educator, poet and scholar known for pioneering work on issues of gender and education in the Kurdistan region of Iraq.

The people's melody

For the first time, English readers can now experience the joys of Ethiopian poetry written in Amharic. The translators of an anthology talk to **MARK FRARY** and, overleaf, we publish a selection of work

ABOVE: Alemu Tebeje, left, and Chris Beckett, who collaborated on the collection

WHEN YOU READ the poems on the pages that follow, it is likely to be your first experience of Ethiopian poetry.

The poems come from Songs We Learn From Trees, the first anthology of Ethiopian Amharic poetry in English – edited and translated by Alemu Tebeje and Chris Beckett. "I once asked a poet friend in Addis why there was so little Ethiopian poetry translated into European languages," said Beckett. "The answer came with an ironic laugh: 'Chris, we suffer because we were never colonised.' The corollary is that Ethiopians are used to being independent, and ignored by the world, and are maybe even grateful for that. They have a rich popular culture which they are proud of, without having to receive confirmation from outside."

LEFT: An orthodox priest in the Gheralta mountains of Tigray, a region caught in conflict again with the government in Addis Ababa

unofficial poet laureate and the other, a co-founder of the first political party in Ethiopia, the Ethiopian People's Revolutionary Party.

In 2018, Carcanet commissioned Beckett and Tebeje to produce the new anthology.

Those new to Amharic poetry might need a primer.

Ethiopia today is made up of more than 80 different language groups, which share a lot of common purposes, stresses and strains. This gives rise

Poetry is mainstream but it often has to express its criticisms obliquely, because of censorship and repercussions

Beckett grew up in Ethiopia in the 1960s and studied languages at Oxford. After more than 30 years in international transport and commodities, he decided to dedicate his time and energy to writing and translating poetry.

He was spurred to promote Ethiopian poetry after buying the Penguin Book of Modern African Poetry only to find that there was not a single Ethiopian poet included.

Ethiopian-born Tebeje, meanwhile, spent his boyhood in Shashemene – the town south of Addis Ababa where Haile Selassie famously welcomed Rastafarians to settle – before studying

Ethiopian languages and literature at Addis Ababa University.

As chief editor for the Ethiopian Science and Technology Commissions journal, he came into increasing conflict with the censorship of the Tigray People's Liberation Front-led government that replaced Haile Mengistu Mariam's military regime in 1991, and he was forced to seek asylum in the UK.

The two ended up working together after Tebeje cleared up Beckett's confusion over finding there were two Ethiopian poets called Tsegaye Gebre Medhin: one, the country's

to two common types of poem – the nationalistic hymn (extolling bravery against outside enemies such as Let Me Dig Up Their Bones by Yoftahe Negussie, which is reproduced here) and the passionate exhortation to ethnic harmony (such as Solomon Deressa's Poem to the Matrix, also in the anthology).

"Poets have long been warning against the dangers of ethnic hatred and division, especially since the TPLF-led government took power in 1991 and changed the centralised system of government to a federal system based on ethnic majorities in each state – with each having large, →

CREDIT: Franck Metois / Alamy Stock Photo

RIGHT: Children at school in Afar, north-east Ethiopia

→ diverse and increasingly persecuted minorities," said Tebeje. "Negussie reminds us of their great victories over Italian and Sudanese invaders and calls for unison against foreign aggression. Implicit in this is the need for cohesion and unity as Ethiopians together."

This resonates at a time of unrest in the country, particularly in Tigray.

He says poetry is mainstream in Ethiopia but that it often has to express its criticisms obliquely, because of censorship and repercussions. "It takes its truth-telling role very seriously."

Asked about the poems printed here, Tebeje said: "Husbands is such an interesting poem. Feminist and playful, personal but very political, and full of memorable images like 'because the lid doesn't fit and the leaders don't fit', which we believe is saying something very profound about the mood of Ethiopians today.

"Ethiopian poets are brilliant at finding new ways to write about corruption," he said, talking about My Continent's Election Song.

"Here Nebiy Mekonnen compares corruption in politics to that in sport. The chants at football matches and election rallies are both underpinned by whippings and beatings of anyone who disagrees."

Beckett said: "We see Zewdu Milikit's The Fashion of Silence as a sort of shame poem – a complaint not only against censorship but against our too-easy acceptance of censorship. It is that rare thing, a poem which criticises itself as well as what it sees as the lies and cowardice the world has come to accept in the interests of comfort, prosperity, a quiet life." ✖

Mark Frary is associate editor at Index on Censorship

50(04):108/111|DOI:10.1177/03064220211068740

Husbands Of My Dear Country

By Mihret Kebede

Let me have a polite conversation with my country
let me write a poem to benefit my country
even if I'm not able to write a poem for my country like the wise poets write
even if I'm not the legal husband of my country or a leader
let me still water the dry land with planted sweat
let me slip in by the fence as a lover
by the front by the top by the upper upper door
they closed the gate but the gate never fits
it never fitted you probably it never properly
fit the bowl and the opening doesn't open doesn't let anyone in
through the place where things don't fit anyway an opening
either way either way I don't want to ask you to marry
instead let me write you a poem
let me fit a poem to benefit my country
collecting the hill of words
the poetry of the people is the melody of the people
until I grow vines I will fit you with my poetry
until I twist lines here I will build a rhyming house here for you
because the lid doesn't fit and the leaders don't fit
and they always leave the door open
they always leave the lid of the pot open
so people can scoop things out scoop things out scoop things out

My Continent's Election Song

By Nebiy Mekonnen

An election in Africa!
a football cup in Africa!
today an election…
today a football match…
on every day, year, country
in my continent
there is a race, a kind of war
through which the same song threads
its warp and weft
its notes composed
of whips
and beatings
into a universal soundtrack, persistently
magnificent
the steady chords and rhythms
like a holy water
springing out
from cellars and from rooftops
gushing this chorus
again again again
it's rigged…
it's rigged…..
it's rigged…….

The Fashion of Silence

By Zewdu Milikit

Our academic beards
grew long and thick,
we never combed our hair.
'I don't need much!'
we'd say, our trousers
thin as hermits'
under our itchy coats.
We discussed
everything that mattered
in the world, tearing
our opinions out like pages

from a breathing book.
But that's all gone:
our hair is slapped with oil
and smartly trimmed,
our leaner bodies
own a rack of shiny epithets,
our shirts and ties
are mute, even our jackets
don a pensive look
but oh! our baggy pants
are loose enough
to hide a thousand secrets
and whisper when we walk.
The temper of the times
has changed, we do not dare
discuss a thing of
all those everythings
that mattered
and still matter in the world –
today our House of Learning
wears a fashionable hush.

Let Me Dig Up Their Bones

By Yoftahe Negussie

Every night I dream of digging up
the graves of Gobena in Shewa,
Alula in Tigray:
Gobena's bones for making bullets,
Alula's bones to make winds whistle.
Put together so they teach Gobena's daughters
how to ride a horse,
Alula's daughters how to fire a gun,
for if our country does not come together
and tuck her toe into the stirrup,
she will be toppled…she will fall off.
Let our four founding fathers,
Mekonnen, Dereso,
Alula and Gobena
teach us how to ride a horse again!
Gobena, rise up with your horse again! ✖

*Songs We Learned From Trees, edited and translated
by **Alemu Tebeje** and **Chris Beckett**, is published by
Carcanet Press (carcanet.co.uk).*

END NOTE

No corruption please, we're British

The UK has developed a parallel vocabulary to avoid labelling anyone with the c-word ... until now, says **OLIVER BULLOUGH**

N TRADITIONAL BRITISH English, the word "corruption" is an irregular noun. This grammatical oddity conjugates thus: I am helping my friends, you are involved in unethical practices, he is engaging in misconduct in public life, a foreigner is guilty of corruption.

This is, in my experience, unique. In other countries I have written about, politicians regularly accuse opponents of corruption, while of course denying it themselves. In Britain, however, we resort to euphemisms: cronyism, paid lobbying, cash-for-questions, sleaze. I do not know anywhere else that seems so determined to insist that corruption is alien to its traditions that it has invented a parallel vocabulary to describe how people abuse their powers.

This is a problem because, by linguistically cutting itself off from the global mainstream, Britain has also stopped itself from learning how other countries have tackled corruption. If British politicians are not corrupt, what relevance does the prosecution of former French president Nicolas Sarkozy have; or the congressional investigation into Donald Trump; or the journalistic investigations into Vladimir Putin?

This autumn, however, thanks to an explosion of allegations, something appears to have changed. In the last six months alone we've heard about ministers creating a special "VIP lane" to allow their contacts to bid for Covid-19-related contracts without the paperwork imposed on ordinary bidders; about MPs lobbying ministers on behalf of private clients; about party donors

receiving peerages in exchange for large donations; about ministers exploiting a loophole in regulations to avoid having to tell the public who's been paying for their holidays; about foreign governments paying for MPs' groups to get around lobbying restrictions.

Opposition parties are now freely using the c-word to describe ministers' behaviour. In the media, even a legal commentator as sober as David Allen Green of the Financial Times has argued that corruption is the best term to describe the assault on the integrity of British institutions staged by Boris Johnson's government.

It's too early to say whether this will be a short-term political phenomenon, or whether it's the start of a realisation that corruption isn't some foreign disease like rabies kept out of Britain by the English Channel. But this awareness is certainly spreading into other spheres. One law enforcement source recently told me that investigators were starting to "turn over the corruption rock to see what's underneath". These are baby steps, but babies grow bigger, and perhaps this will too.

It's hard to overstate how important it could be if Brits realised they're not immune to corruption and began to treat it as the threat to civilisation that it is. London has, for decades, been the most popular adopted home for the world's crooks and thieves and, thanks to Britain's traditional reluctance to label its own as corrupt, they have been able to enjoy the hospitality of the city unchallenged. By gifting small fractions

ABOVE: Owen Paterson, the former MP for North Shropshire, who resigned in November over sleaze/corruption allegations

of their stolen wealth to universities, galleries, charities and – sometimes – even politicians, they have become "philanthropists", "entrepreneurs" or "socialites". Journalists are then unable to write the truth about them, because it's defamatory to be rude about a philanthropist. And that means financial institutions have been happy to move their money around, because – well – what reason would they have not to?

Britain has acted as a huge loophole through which corrupt money has poured into the global economy; blocking that hole is the biggest service Brits could do for the world. I am hopeful that the transformation of "corruption" into a word that can describe the behaviour of British politicians as well as foreigners, and the recognition that this blight affects us as much as anyone, is a step towards that. ✖

Oliver Bullough is the author of Moneyland: Why Thieves and Crooks Now Rule the World

50(04):112/112|DOI:10.1177/03064220211068741